THE LIVE E-LEARNING COOKBOOK

The Live E-Learning Cookbook

Recipes for Success

Kathleen Barclay, Ph.D.
Al Gordon
Jim Hollahan
Yatman Lai

iUniverse, Inc.
New York Lincoln Shanghai

The Live E-Learning Cookbook
Recipes for Success

iUniverse, Inc.

For information address:
iUniverse, Inc.
2021 Pine Lake Road, Suite 100
Lincoln, NE 68512
www.iuniverse.com

ISBN: 0-595-27667-9

Printed in the United States of America

Contents

Preface

Live e-learning in a virtual classroom brings together the best of in-person instruction, the power of social learning, and the scalability and dynamic power of the Internet. We are four training executives who understand the competitive advantage of a skilled, knowledgeable workforce. We believe that an effective and scalable strategy for updating employee skills, knowledge, and abilities, is *real time, instructor-led live e-learning*.

The Live E-learning Cookbook is written for business managers and trainers responsible for creating and delivering employee training programs to meet three key business challenges:

1. **Time to Market—How rapidly can I deploy new products?**

2. **Time to Productivity—How rapidly can I deploy new skills?**

3. **Time to Knowledge—How rapidly can I disseminate information?**

This cookbook is written to help you achieve these goals through successful e-learning employee training programs.

WHY THIS COOKBOOK?

Managers are asking if there is a better way to combine existing self-paced e-learning with enterprise wide training strategies. Companies are discovering the high development costs and high dropout rates of self-paced training. Employees need more than self-paced courses when learning new business practices. Jay Cross and Lance Dublin reported at TechLearn 2002 that:

- 31%—the number of people that do not sign up for mandatory e-learning.

- 68%—the number that do not show up for voluntary e-learning.

- 50–80%—commonly experienced dropout rates.

In other words, Cross and Dublin conclude that *if you build it, they may not come.*

Another common concern for business managers is finding an alternative that reduces travel costs and time out of the office for employee training and new product instructions.

Live virtual classroom-based e-learning combines the best of classroom training with web-based instruction, providing scalability and expanding the *anywhere* advantage. Live e-learning includes personal interaction and collaboration that keep employees coming back. Live e-learning enables managers to provide a new mix of learning opportunities directed at bottom line business results, while also breaking barriers of high development costs, distance, and time away from the worksite.

BUSINESS CHALLENGES

Managers are continually searching for a better way of combining existing communication with training that will yield better results at a lower cost. You may already be researching alternatives that would help you effectively reduce travel and meeting budgets and time out of the office while still effectively meeting your business objectives. This cookbook is written for you—to help you implement successful e-learning in your company.

You should read this book:

1. When, as a **curious learner**, you are trying to discover *what is live e-learning*. Read and scan this book for basic information.

2. When, as a **business executive**, you are trying to decide if live e-learning is right for your company. Find concrete examples to help you better understand how live e-learning will work to get better business results.

3. When, as a **business manager** or **training director** whose company has already made the commitment to employ live e-learning, you are trying to understand how to go forward. Discover valuable and practical solutions for how to use the new technology to rapidly address urgent training needs.

CHAPTER ORGANIZATION

"Now that my company has purchased e-learning software or made arrangements to access software through a hosting company, how do I use this new training tool to get maximum business results for my organization?"

To help you answer this question, information is organized into concise, easy-to-read chapters, each providing a summary of our experience and many tips and techniques for developing e-learning solutions. We have included **COOKBOOK QUESTIONS** throughout the chapters to help you plan dynamic projects.

We have formatted this cookbook to provide you with the elements to rapidly plan, design, and deploy live e-learning solutions that address your specific business needs—use what is best for your situation. **COOKBOOK SCENARIOS** of actual applications are included in each chapter to stimulate your thinking and show you a variety of ways that companies have used live e-learning.

By the way, this is not a cookbook for how to buy technology. In writing this book, we assume that you have already made a purchase or hosting decision for one of a variety of live e-learning virtual classrooms that are currently on the market. If you are trying to make a purchase decision, you will find helpful resources and references. Our goal is to share **COOKBOOK KEY POINTS** and techniques we have developed over the years to provide you with a guide to rapidly learn the ins and outs of this new and powerful virtual classroom.

HOW TO USE THIS RESOURCE

To take full advantage of this Cookbook you should expect to spend time with the information, scenarios, and resources you will find here.

1. You will need to read, gather information, and reflect.

2. To begin to apply this information most effectively, we strongly encourage both business unit managers and training managers to read this book.

3. You will need time to discuss the information you find here with your co-workers. You will be introduced to new ideas and concepts about training. You will need to talk about and test out those concepts in order to see how they apply in your company.

4. Finally, you will need to begin developing a plan for your first pilot project.

SUMMARY

It has been our pleasure to put this Cookbook together. We have developed a strong commitment to the work we do with live e-learning. This book is our effort to share our experience with you. We have worked with a wide range of companies who have achieved exciting learning results with the successful application of principles we cover in this book. Have fun with this learning experience!

COOKBOOK QUESTION

Write down the details of a current and urgent training challenge. Stated another way, write down your current *what keeps you up at night* business problem.

To maximize your use of this Cookbook, refer back to this business problem as you read through the following chapters.

1. Briefly describe your business challenge.

2. What is the current situation? Describe current performance.

3. What changes in performance would you like to achieve?

4. Who are the stakeholders?

1

What You Should Know

WHAT IS LIVE E-LEARNING?

Live e-learning—also known as synchronous learning, the virtual class-room, or online instructor-led training—uses specialized software in combination with phone capability or voice-over-Internet-protocol (VOIP) to add an interactive dimension to instruction delivered via a web browser over the Internet or an intranet. Participants benefit from real-time interactive strategies such as collaboration, practice and application, demonstration, debate, questions, or discussion. The virtual classroom takes the best of the traditional classroom—talking with each other and with the instructor, viewing slides, asking questions, working in small groups—and turbo-charges it to provide learners separated by geography with professional training that might otherwise not be available.

On the following page, you will find a chart comparing traditional training with self-paced e-learning and live e-learning modalities. Note how the learner and instructor roles change as the format for learning delivery changes.

LEARNING MODALITIES COMPARED

Traditional Training

Learner	Directed
Instructor	Teacher
Time	Scheduled
Facility	Physical room

Self-Paced E-Learning

Learner	Self-directed
Instructor	Not involved
Time	Anytime
Facility	Anywhere

Live E-Learning

Learner	Guided
Instructor	Facilitator
Time	Scheduled
Facility	Web-based

ADVANTAGES OF LIVE E-LEARNING

Several main factors are important to the recent development of web-based e-learning:

- Easy or fast access to new information
- Time to market for new products
- Improvement of workforce effectiveness and productivity
- Access to subject matter experts who have no time to travel
- Reduction of training and operating expenses
- Need to increase employee retention.

Live e-learning provides a number of competitive advantages for you and your company:

LIVE E-LEARNING CLASSROOM ADVANTAGES

Interactivity
Employees have the opportunity to ask questions, test their assumptions, practice techniques, and participate in discussions with subject matter experts.

Motivational Learning Experiences
Employees learn from colleagues by collaborating and competing with colleagues.

Rapid Content Development
Documents and class activity slides are readily developed or adapted—low development time and cost.

Collaboration and Team Building
Facilitates team building and reduces the learning curve for sales and work teams.

Quick Turnaround

Opportunity to introduce new skills and provides participants with on the job practice and support as those skills are acquired.

Instant Feedback

Students can ask questions and dialogue with the instructor. Through dialogue the instructor gets feedback on how well students have understood the material.

STRATEGIC ADVANTAGES

Geographic Reach

The virtual classroom rapidly reaches dispersed employees at great cost savings. Leverage the productivity of regularly scheduled face-to-face meetings by conducting virtual class sessions before or after these meetings.

Rapid Deployment

The low-tech one or two telephone line solution shortens the time required to get information and skill training to employees and/or customers.

Increased Flexibility

Information can be targeted to specific work groups. Employees can be reached in small groups regardless of their geographic locations.

Scales to Large Meetings

Informational presentations can be made by executive or product management.

Scales for Small Classes

Provides skills training in small, highly interactive groups.

Enables on the Job Practice

Allows for a series of short class sessions scheduled over time, permitting practice between sessions and ongoing access for subject matter expert assistance.

To illustrate these advantages, let us review a real business problem that was solved using the live e-learning classroom.

COOKBOOK SCENARIO

CRM Software

The Challenge

A large computer company was faced with the challenge of rolling out a new Customer Relationship Management (CRM) software package for over 500 sales people nationwide. The Training Department was given responsibility to manage the nationwide rollout. The sales department included multiple business units and 500+ employees dispersed throughout the United States and Canada. Sales executives worked from both home and company offices.

The business case for the company was:

- Improved contact management system—one system for the entire company.

- Better management and coordination of business prospects.

- Improved tracking and follow up, better coordination on complex sales.

- Improved reporting of sales opportunities in the sales funnel.

- Improved management access to sale funnel information.

- Better coordination with manufacturing and inventory to meet anticipated sales.

- Ability for sales teams to share leads and complex sales.

- Better coordination with vendors and sales partner organizations.

The business outcomes for the salesperson:

- Sales divisions in the company were using different CRM systems.

- There was a willingness to change because the current CRM systems fell short of expectations.

- Sales people were also skeptical because earlier versions were excessively promoted.

- New CRM tracking and sharing features were tools sales people saw as valuable for managing contacts, opportunities, and their sales funnel.

- Everyone was clear on the company wide deadline and commitment to the implementation of the new system. There was no turning back.

The Training Solution

In order to meet an aggressive CRM software rollout plan, it was impossible to consider any type of face-to-face training plan. Travel costs and time restraints made a face-to-face training solution impractical.

The company developed a project website and provided a range of informational and reference documents on the new CRM software. An offline CRM training database was established and a 90-minute virtual training program introducing the new software was developed. The critical *must know* software navigation and operational features were identified and covered in this introductory training. The company already had virtual classroom software installed on their corporate network. A training team of six trainers worked out the strategy for using the training database and application sharing to demonstrate the basic operational and navigation features of the new software.

Classes were scheduled over a three-week period for groups of up to 25 sales people. The master schedule offered classes at different times during the day to make the classes accessible for sales people in different time zones. Once the master schedule was developed, different sales divisions were assigned a group of classes. Sales people from that group could enroll in any of the classes in that group.

CRM Virtual Classroom Training Program Design

The CRM training was delivered in a 90 minute virtual class session, each attended by 20 to 25 sales executives. The outline for the 90 minute class was as follows:

> *Part I—Basic training in the software operations—60 minutes*

- CRM Overview—using slides on the whiteboard

- Demo/Training of CRM software using application sharing

> *Part II—Hands-on Forecasting Lab—30 minutes*

- Forecasting Lab. The Lab was conducted online with the instructors providing audio support. The sales reps received their passwords and signed on to the new CRM Database. They reviewed their account data that was migrated from other Legacy systems, entered new opportunities and submitted their first sales forecast practicing the new skills they had learned.

Performance Outcome

Each sales person submitted an initial monthly sales funnel status report at the end of the training. Sales Managers reviewed the test reports and followed up individually with those sales executives who did not successfully submit a report.

Support materials for the training included:

- End-user website that contained all communication and documentation
- Online registration at the end-user website
- *Read Me First* Instructions
- Reference Guide
- Quick Reference Card
- Standard Business Processes Guide.

Following the online training, each sales person had to complete his or her first monthly sales forecast on the new CRM system within the next two weeks. Sales forecasts were automatically sent to the sales managers, so there was a system in place to check on and follow up for sales people who had difficulty with the software operation.

The Result

Five hundred sales people made the successful transition to the new CRM system on the date that the new CRM software database went *live*.

COOKBOOK KEY POINTS

The previous scenario illustrates the power of a well-designed live e-learning program in addressing a very complex training challenge. As a business unit or training manager deciding what the right design is for an e-learning solution to your business problem, you will want useful information to help make that decision. Throughout this book, we will provide **Cookbook Key Points** for you to consider. Let us start with the following key points:

'One size' does not fit all learning needs.

Ask yourself:

- How complex is the learning task? Is it a question of communicating basic information or does the learning outcome require complex skills and practice?

- Is the learning task straightforward, logical, and information rich? Or will learners encounter a variety of questions as they learn the material? One of the limitations of using only self-paced learning is that learners often do not have access to the subject matter expert if they have questions about the content or its application in a business situation.

Consider implementing 'blended learning'.

A blended learning program is defined as the combination of a variety of learning formats appropriately used to best achieve the required business result. Examples of blending would be live-e-learning:

- Combined with self-paced class sessions
- Combined with face-to-face training
- Combined with on the job practice
- Combined with coaching or mentoring
- Combined with virtual team learning exercises.

In the corporate world, focus is on learning outcomes rather than on a particular technology delivery system. Good e-learning design takes advantage of a variety of e-learning delivery methods and focuses on the most time- and cost-effective strategies that have the highest probability of achieving your desired business outcomes.

THE COOKBOOK BENEFIT: ACHIEVE BOTTOM LINE RESULTS

Managers typically are tasked with five general responsibilities for which the live e-learning classroom can be an important tool:

- Information transfer
- Performance improvement
- Skills development
- Product launches and updates
- Getting people to think differently.

Your company can use live e-learning to help maximize business results for e-information, e-communication, e-collaboration, and e-training to address business challenges such as:

Information Transfer

- Broadcast communications to large, dispersed audiences
- Partner or investor briefings
- Webinars and seminars
- Subject matter expert briefings
- Product update briefings.

Performance Improvement

- Human Resources training, benefits and/or procedures
- Software training
- Enterprise training (SAP or CRM system training)
- Workplace safety and governmental regulations compliance
- Management and leadership training

- Six Sigma and other quality improvement systems
- Balanced Scorecard or other training for managers.

Skill Development

- New employee orientation training
- Global training (multiple people across the globe on same team)
- Skills training involving small, highly interactive, learning exercises
- Pre-training preparation and introduction of materials for face-to-face classes
- Live virtual class components to self-paced training
- Train-the-trainer
- Process re-engineering training
- Training on contracts and legal requirements.

Product Launch—Product Updates

- Sales training
- Marketing programs
- Product training for resellers
- Product training for customers
- Technical support
- Account management
- New product launches
- Sales presentations
- How to submit proposal and bids
- Customer service.

Getting People to Think Differently

- Virtual class follow-up to face-to-face meetings to support application of new skills on the job as well as follow-up coaching and support sessions

- Project management and coordination.

COOKBOOK QUESTION

What business problem are you trying to address with a training solution?

In your company, which of the business challenges listed in this chapter could benefit from using live e-learning to help improve business results?

- Information transfer
- Performance improvement
- Skill development
- Product launches
- Product updates
- Getting people to think differently

Other challenges your company is facing:

COOKBOOK SCENARIO

Telecommunications Sales Training

The Challenge

A large telecommunications company needed to continuously update 2,500 North American sales representatives on voice and data products and services, and on newly launched offerings. Classroom-based instruction consumed a large part of the training budget. Travel, instructor, and facilities costs were high. Classes were hard to schedule to keep everyone informed in a timely manner.

The Solution

The company began looking for web-based learning options. After contracting with a firm that develops customized e-learning solutions, an e-learning website was operational within eight weeks. The site featured materials and product information. New products were announced using a combination of classroom and live online seminars, complete with presentations by Product Managers. Sales Managers got instant feedback on the learning progress of their staff. Sales reps used their mobile phones to receive updates. Streaming audio was used for distribution of key management update messages and allowed for case studies (archived after the live session) to be available for sales representative review.

The Result

The company trained nearly half of the field sales force by the end of the first month rather than the two months it typically took to train the same number of people using a classroom. Reducing multiple classroom sessions lowered training costs. The three-day seminar was changed into a one-day class with online training as a prerequisite, thereby reducing time out of the field by two days and saving travel costs. The online solution provided a net savings of $100,000 per new product launch.

2

Building the Foundation

"For learners, how extensively the course was marketed and promoted was the single most influential factor for increasing the likelihood that learners would begin the course."

Source: Internet Time Group

DEFINE YOUR BUSINESS CASE

Research has shown that about 1/3 of all learners fail to register for mandatory e-learning and almost 70% fail to register for voluntary e-learning. You do not want this to happen with your project. As you begin to implement your dynamic training program, use the following information to help build a successful foundation for your live e-learning initiative.

Defining the business case is your first step in creating any training program, including live e-learning. Here are some suggestions for building your business case:

- Develop a business plan that can be easily conveyed to executives, managers, and supervisors.

- Relate the program to strategic business direction.

- Manage expectations up front regarding the importance of the program, participation requirements, and performance expectations.

- Hold managers accountable for the success of their employees in keeping with company objectives and expectations.

COOKBOOK KEY POINT

Success will result from careful planning that is aligned with company direction.

E-learning is particularly suited to today's need for rapid dissemination of knowledge and information, especially when offices are separated by geography and multiple time zones. We have advanced a long way since the days of the first correspondence courses in the 1800s. We moved through educational radio and then television in the 1900s to our current use of technology learning solutions. Today's technologies include satellite, video, audio teleconferencing, CD, and most recently, web-based e-learning. This chapter provides information about the essential elements you must consider as you plan, develop, and implement your business plan for live e-learning.

Attention to e-learning fundamentals will help you develop your business case. E-learning enables you to more easily compare your *expected* learner outcomes with your *realized* learner outcomes. E-learning will help your company achieve breakthrough results by:

- Reducing cycle times.
- Improving the productivity of sales channels.
- Helping customers become smarter buyers.
- Aligning the workforce with current corporate strategy.
- Launching new products and services globally.
- Rolling out enterprise systems such as CRM or ERP.
- Re-skilling workers to execute new business processes.

COOKBOOK SCENARIO

SAP Implementation

The Challenge

The corporation needed to train 120 financial administration employees on the new SAP general ledger system. Expense constraints precluded flying everyone into headquarters. Wide dispersion of most of the employees made it impractical to fly instructors to 50+ locations where only one or two employees worked. Due to the mission critical nature of this financial application, it was determined that self-paced training was too risky. It was decided that live contact with SAP subject matter experts was required to ensure that employees were comfortable with the new system.

The Solution

The live virtual classroom allowed employees to participate in the training from their offices without having to travel. The instructors/subject matter experts conducted the classes from headquarters, allowing them to continue their normal work responsibilities in addition to teaching. Instructors sent the SAP training manual to the students for review two weeks prior to the live virtual classroom training.

Two live class sessions of two hours in length were conducted. Class size was limited to ten to allow for individualized instruction. The instructor used the whiteboard tool to show slides of key points and screen captures of various SAP application components. At various points in the class, the instructor used application sharing to demonstrate the SAP client. Students also logged on to their SAP server and replicated the instructor's actions. If the students ran into difficulty, they shared their application with the class and the instructor could correct their actions.

The virtual classroom was used in conjunction with audio conferencing. The key technical component was the application sharing feature. This allowed both the instructor and the students to share their desktops and work with the live SAP application (using a practice database).

The Result

All 120 employees became proficient on the SAP application in a thirty-day period. Travel costs in excess of $160,000 were avoided. Lost productivity of 300 person-days was avoided, saving the soft dollar cost estimated at $400,000.

TRAINING COST SAVINGS

Live e-learning significantly reduces training budgets by eliminating the cost of instructor and/or student travel and classroom facilities. While this will help you justify your project, a more significant cost and time savings is minimizing time away from work. Live e-learning:

- **Eliminates travel costs for instructors and students**—Costs include airfare, mileage, and lodging, and employee wages while on travel.

- **Reduces training induced productivity loss**—Live e-learning programs, if designed properly, are easily integrated into the participants work schedule.

- **Reduces number of instructors**—The same instructor can deliver more training sessions within the same period of time. As a result, you will need fewer instructors to cover the same number of students.

- **Reduces course development cost**—Live e-learning can leverage the same materials commonly used in classroom training.

This represents a huge savings when compared to other forms of custom e-learning.

COOKBOOK SCENARIO

Technology Training

The Challenge

A major technology company had developed and delivered a successful two-day instructor-led, lecture/lab training course. A tight economy meant limited travel and training budgets, creating an emphasis on reducing costs, increasing employee productivity, and imposing severe time constraints for technical staff. The company needed to find a more cost-effective and accelerated way to deliver this critical information to its technical employees. Feedback from previous e-learning courses indicated that these technical employees liked the flexibility of modularized, self-paced, e-learning. However, they still wanted the opportunity to learn from their peers and gain access to a content expert, the type of activities that occur in the traditional face-to-face environment.

The Solution

An approach was developed that intelligently repackaged, not recreated, the existing content into a hybrid, live/self-paced training solution. This course blended the best of both worlds using the following components:

- A 40-minute pre-course streaming video introducing the course.

- Three, two-hour, live virtual classroom sessions led by a subject matter expert.

- Five e-labs (multimedia-based lab simulations) with specific tasks to be accomplished per lab to demonstrate the content.

- Several interactive, self-paced modules were scheduled between the live sessions. These combined rich multimedia tools such as animation and streaming video demonstrations.

- Assessments after each module via an online testing application evaluated comprehension of the material.

The Result

The 20 employees attending the first course gave it an average rating of 4.47 out of 5, an excellent score. Eighty percent of these students rated the course better than previously offered streaming video self-paced training. Two-thirds of the students felt that it was equal to or better than classroom training because the material was focused and the format eliminated the need for travel.

The self-paced aspects of the blended course enabled learners to work at their own pace while the virtual classroom sessions provided highly interactive discussion with the subject matter experts. One hundred percent of the participating employees agreed that the company should offer more courses like it. Commented one student, "If it is up to me, I will never take a classroom course again. This type of training is GREAT."

The return-on-investment for the course was substantial. In terms of hard dollar savings associated with eliminating a four-day trip, the company estimated an average $2,100 savings per employee for airfare, lodging, car, meals, and miscellaneous expenses.

Soft dollar savings of field productivity are based on the assumption that the employee remains primarily in the field while taking the class instead of missing four days of work out of 235 work days per year, or 1.7 percent of each student's annual productivity. Assuming that an employee's average benefits-loaded salary is $144,000 per year, soft-dollar productivity savings per student per day average $613 or $2,452 for four days.

The combined estimated hard and soft dollar savings of the hybrid e-learning course totaled $4,552 per student. If, for example, twelve classes with 20 employees each are delivered, 240 employees will attend the training program. A cost saving of $4,552 per employee results in a $1,092,480 annual savings for the course. A five-year analysis estimated that an investment of $150,000 would return $5,312,400.

COOKBOOK KEY POINT

Reserve a portion of your hard dollar cost savings to cover new costs (software, telecommunications, support) of developing and deploying live e-learning programs.

BUSINESS VALUE

Beyond saving costs, this new mode of learning delivery provides a powerful tool for the organization to compete effectively in the global market.

SHORTEN NEW PRODUCT TIME TO MARKET

Increase speed of course creation

Live e-learning allows you to use standard presentation file formats and leverage most of the communications and product information collateral (presentations, websites, brochures).

Deliver training quickly

Live e-learning eliminates the need to deliver training geographically, thus enabling you to deliver training to those who need it most regardless of physical location.

Reach large audiences quickly

The size of a live e-learning class is limited only by your design and the capacity of the software platform. When properly designed, live e-learning can reach your target audience world-wide in a matter of days instead of weeks or months.

DECREASE TIME TO KNOWLEDGE AND SKILL

Subject matter expert participation

Live e-learning allows subject matter experts to lead most of the training sessions from their desks. Dialogue between SMEs and participants provides instant feedback on your learning program and allows for real-time adjustments in the training content. Since SMEs can participate as instructors, the need for train-the-trainer programs can be reduced or eliminated.

Engaging student-learning experience

Students attribute higher satisfaction to a live e-learning program because of the spontaneous exchanges of ideas between instructors (typically subject matter experts) and participants, and among the participants themselves.

Effective performance support

Small group post-training follow-up sessions can provide further guidance and support as employees apply new skills and knowledge in the actual work environment.

COOKBOOK SCENARIO

Reseller Communication

The Challenge

This Internet Company made sales through a worldwide network of affiliate resellers, who provided a variety of telecommunications services to customers. To better serve the many resellers located all over the globe, the Professional Services Group was responsible for providing ongoing consulting and training services. Their mission included communicating important new product information to all of the company's resellers in a timely manner. English was not the first language for many of the international resellers and much of the new product information was complex.

The Professional Services Group had eight or more instructors traveling world wide to provide product update trainings. In early 2000, the group began looking for a solution that would allow them to present information more effectively and efficiently than sending instructors out to the global offices.

The Solution

The Professional Services Group selected a synchronous virtual classroom product that provided the collaboration and presentation power they needed. They chose an Application Service Provider (ASP) who could supply outsourced virtual classroom services that easily integrated into the company's network infrastructure. The visual and interactive aspects of the virtual classroom made it much easier for international resellers to better understand the subject matter. Instructors used graphics to clearly explain complex ideas to those for whom English is not their first language.

The Result

The Professional Services Group enjoyed increased efficiency because it could now provide quality support to its resellers in far less time, with reduced travel. Virtual classroom trainings achieved learning results similar to face-to-face trainings and could be deployed much more rapidly.

The group also discovered just how practical the live online application was for other purposes. They conducted a very large training conference in New York and had planned to send one of the executives to address the audience. However, at the last moment, a conflict arose that made it impossible for the executive to make the trip to New York. The virtual classroom was used effectively to give a great one-hour presentation—a very practical solution for resolving time and schedule constraints.

COOKBOOK QUESTION

What should success look like when you include live e-learning in your training strategy? Take a few minutes to make notes here on your vision of success. Think about what success will look like when your ideas are fully implemented.

What does your program look like?

What results do you want to achieve?

SETTING EXPECTATIONS

Setting expectations correctly beforehand is crucial to acceptance. Tell employees about the training. They will want to know *what's in it for me* (the WIIFM).

The invitation should concentrate on the same business benefits that resonate with managers—productivity savings and more effective learning. Your announcements and descriptions should be concise, easy to understand, provide complete details about the training, and motivate employees to actively participate. Accentuate the positives! Items to cover include:

- **Course objectives**—This is a great way to dispel any misconception about the effectiveness of live e-learning. It should be results-oriented, not technology-driven. Remember, employees may be wowed by the whiz-bang technology, but if the content does not meet their needs, it is futile.

- **Participation requirements**—This is especially important if you are offering a multi-session class and/or a blended class (including self-paced materials). Provide time estimates that include live classroom time with pre and post assignments.

- **Equipment checklist**—Learners must verify that they have access to computers that meet minimum requirements prior to registering for the class. Procedures for conducting system checks, browser tests, and installation of any plug-ins or client software installations must be provided. Provide sources on how to acquire necessary software and hardware. Make sure this is a student responsibility.

- **Learning environment**—Provide tips on how to create a learning environment that blocks out distractions and interruptions. This includes getting management support.

- **Technical support**—Provide web links and phone numbers on how to seek technical support if encountering equipment or connection problems. Encourage students to check their equipment prior to class.

- **Instruction**—Distribute clear directions on how to come to class and quick reference cards for features and procedures students will need to know for successful participation in class.

- **Acknowledge success**—Award a certificate, diploma of completion, or other public recognition to employees when completing the course. Some companies have found that simple mementos such as coffee mugs, t-shirts, or golf hats have been very effective for promoting and acknowledging participation in a new e-learning program.

COOKBOOK KEY POINT

Do not overlook the instructors/subject matter experts —they must be sold on the medium as well.

MARKETING LIVE E-LEARNING

The challenge of marketing your live e-learning offerings lies in getting your learners and appropriate managers excited about it. Nothing is more important than getting line manager support for the participants when the delivery system is relatively new. Since training is being delivered primarily to the point of work, you must create a supportive environment for employees to attend the training.

- **Send the announcement to managers first**—This early communication needs to explain the reason for live e-learning, describe the learning experience, student benefits, and business outcomes.

- **Conduct a live demo for key managers**—There is nothing like experiencing live e-learning to be convinced that it is a better way to train. Once managers are convinced that it is a serious learning tool, they are more likely to support and provide the right environment for employees to participate.

- **Get management feedback**—Line managers are a great source of input for what is workable in their employees' workplace. Verify your assumptions for schedules, equipment, environment, and technical skills.

Now that the managers are convinced about the efficacy of live e-learning, you can concentrate on getting the employees to the class.

COOKBOOK QUESTION

Which points in this chapter do you think are most important to address for your training project?

3

Measuring Business Results

Continuous improvement is a part of any business that represents a significant expenditure of funds by the organization. The pressures of cost cutting, scarce resources, and highly competitive industries have led to increased pressure to verify outcomes. Most executives want to know what impact their departments, programs, and services have with partners, clients, consumers, and customers. Evaluate your e-learning initiative for program productivity and employee performance.

For your company

- Good economic sense
- Provide useful insight to improve quality
- Justify current programs
- Plan for future programs.

For the learner

- Validate learner's involvement
- Overcome fear or apprehension of training
- Verify learning transfer.

COOKBOOK QUESTION

Why are you implementing live online e-learning in your company—be specific.

As you read this chapter, note how you want to evaluate your program to verify desired business results.

USING LEVELS OF EVALUATION

For 40 years, one of the most widely accepted models for measuring the impact of training has been Kirkpatrick's Four Levels of Evaluation. Kirkpatrick's levels measure outcomes from a participant, trainer, and corporate perspective.

Level I

What are participant reactions to the training and what do they plan to do with the class materials?

At the first level, you are probably most familiar with the 'smile sheet' surveys and questionnaires handed out at the end of a course.

Level II

What skills, knowledge, or attributes have been changed or acquired with the training, and to what extent?

The second level involves methods to determine pre- and post-tests or observations.

Level III

Did participants apply what they learned in training to their jobs?

At the third level, an attempt is made to see if course learning is applied in the workplace.

Level IV

Did the on the job application produce measurable results?

The fourth level seeks to verify business results from the training.

Although most current evaluation is conducted at the first two levels, savvy executives increasingly are requesting Level III and IV assessments to gauge the impact of e-learning.

COOKBOOK KEY POINT

Improve the perception of your program's business value by measuring expectations.

When line managers request training, ask about what they expect to get from the training in percentage of improvement or dollar value on performance. In addition to generating more support for the training, managers then have a predisposed interest in the results.

Learner expectations for how they will be able to apply the training to their job can be added to an end of the course evaluation sheet. A follow up survey or interview can then compare original expectations with what they experience as actual outcomes on the job. When employees are honestly asked to take part in the process, they can be very accurate about reporting the resulting figures.

COOKBOOK QUESTION

Which levels of evaluation do you currently use? How satisfactory are your results?

Level I—End of training session evaluations

Level II—Pre and post tests on knowledge and skills

Level III—Assessments of how learning is applied on the job

Level IV—Business results from the training

EVALUATING TRAINING PROGRAM PRODUCTIVITY

Training productivity rates are often measured by criteria such as hours and costs of development time, numbers of students, and hours of training delivered. But, consider this:

> If Project Delta reports 25 hours of course development time for one hour of learning, and Project Plato reports 50 hours of development time for one hour of learning, Project Delta may be judged as more efficient in developing the course. However, if 100 participants in Project Delta finish the training with no observable improvement in performance during the next 6 months, and the 100 participants in the training for Project Plato end up reducing time spent on their learned task by three hours a month and achieve improve performance results on the job—then Project Plato recouped its development cost much more effectively than Project Delta. In this situation, which project would you want to be associated with?

As a business performance improvement tool, building evaluation components into your e-learning program can drive you toward measurable business goals. Following are several useful program evaluation criteria. Which are important for your initiative?

Output

- Number of people (customers, employees, partners) receiving training
- Number of courses deployed
- Total training time/days
- Business results achieved.

Input

- Complexity of material and training design

- Subject matter expert availability

- Instructor expertise levels.

Cost

- Cost of development tools

- Learning curve required for development tools

- Outsourcing to training vendors or consultants

- Amount of existing content re-purposed

- Travel expenses of student/instructors

- Cost of incentives

- Tuition reimbursement.

COOKBOOK QUESTION

Which of these output, input, and cost criteria could you use to evaluate your specific project or program?

Are you missing evaluation processes that would help you better make those decisions?

Is the current method of outcome and productivity assessment what you want it to be?

EVALUATING EMPLOYEE PERFORMANCE

So how do you know if your training makes a difference? Listed below are assessment methods you can use to verify that your virtual classroom training is getting the expected results you want.

Assess if one or more of the following methods can be included into your projects to gain information about the quality, efficiency, and effectiveness of your live online sessions. Then use this information to enhance or improve your program.

- Tests—Give a test in a written form to verify retention of content.

- Observation—Be specific about who observes and what is being observed to verify on the job application of content.

- Questionnaires—Ask for information about your program's effectiveness.

- Management feedback—Ask for information about how management perceives any results and provide them with ways to reinforce what employees learned.

- Peer feedback—Get information on what works and what could be improved.

- Interviews—Talk with employees to find out what they think about the course.

- Attitude surveys—Survey and compile the responses to find patterns.

- Testimonials—Get comments from those who really learned something from the course.

- Expectation versus outcome percents—Compare what you expected with what you see resulting.

- Focus groups—Discussion groups help you identify strengths and weaknesses of the training.

Use a Learning Contract (see the Chapter on developing live e-learning for more information on this method) to verify your learning program outcomes. Make a point of following up with each participant to discuss what they contracted to do with the training and what has resulted.

COOKBOOK QUESTION

Once you have evaluation data, work out how to use it constructively:

1. What will you personally do with the feedback responses to improve the training program?

2. How can you package the findings into a report for management that will gain you support?

3. How will employees have access to the findings while honoring confidentiality?

4

Selecting Your Virtual Classroom

As someone interested in selecting a virtual classroom system for your organization, you will be confronted with several key decision factors. In this chapter we will discuss each of these factors in detail. This chapter will help address following questions and make the best technology decision for your organization.

- What are the virtual classroom features that I need to meet my organization's unique requirements?

- Should I buy or rent a virtual classroom?

- How do I balance a particular virtual classroom system's richness of feature set versus the complexity of the software application installation and support?

- Should I use traditional telephone conference calls versus the less expensive Internet telephony conference?

- What is involved in recording and archiving live e-learning sessions for later viewing?

- Should I use streaming video?

Selecting a virtual classroom in today's environment is a complex, but not impossible task. Each vendor offers a wide variety of features and functionality. To find the right system for you, do your homework, both in terms of what each vendor offers and what you need. If you feel overwhelmed, hire a professional to help. It will be money well spent.

COOKBOOK KEY POINT

It is possible to use a system without the risky purchase decision. The cost of acquisition in terms of capital dollars and labor to set-up a virtual classroom is fairly large. Pay-per-use and ASP approaches are good, conservative, initial steps.

At one time or another you will see a number of products and technologies associated with live e-learning, also sometimes referred to as synchronous learning technology or:

- Virtual Classroom
- Data Conferencing
- Web Conferencing
- Web Casting
- Video Conferencing
- Audio Conferencing
- Streaming (Audio and/or Video)
- Whiteboard Systems.

While all of these technologies are excellent for information distribution and virtual collaboration, some technologies do not provide the level of interaction, instructor control, or richness of presentation to be considered true interactive e-learning technologies. Web casting and streaming, for example, are closer to traditional broadcasting in that they usually involve a larger audience and do not provide for a high level of much student interaction, if at all.

Technologies such as web conferencing or data conferencing often feature peer-to-peer communication and are commonly used for collaboration, team meetings, and work sessions. While these technologies can be used for live e-learning, they only have limited instructor control features and learning management functionality.

KEY ELEMENTS OF THE VIRTUAL CLASSROOM

Throughout the Live E-Learning Cookbook we will use a definition of a live e-learning system that contains several key elements. The students and instructor connect to the virtual classroom using a PC. Most common would be a PC running the Windows© operating system. Some, but not all live e-learning systems will support other operating systems. This is something to check out carefully if your student population uses non-Windows© systems.

Another key element of our definition is that the Internet or an intranet is used as the communications infrastructure. It is becoming increasingly rare to see dedicated, dial-in systems, so we will focus on the Internet Protocol (IP) world.

One trend in client-server computing is the increasing use of the web browser for the client. This use of a *thin client* is often based on the installation of a plug-in or a Java applet program into the browser. On the opposite end of the spectrum is the *thick client* which is a separate, full-blown program installed on the client PC. There are strengths and weaknesses to both approaches. We will discuss this in more detail later in this chapter.

Audio is a critical element of live e-learning. Some systems rely on text-based synchronous communication. However, we will focus on systems that support at least one-way audio from the instructor, and ideally, two-way audio. Audio functionality can be provided through a separate, but simultaneous conference call over the regular telephone network. Audio can also be provided using integrated or separate IP audio. Audio will be covered in more detail later on in this chapter.

The final key element of our live e-learning system is that the instructor or subject matter expert controls the learning environment. The system allows the leader to control the various features of the virtual classroom. This differs from the peer-based systems where everyone has equal control.

COOKBOOK SCENARIO

Project Tracking

The Challenge

A large consulting firm needed to train 900 people in various locations on a new project tracking application. The IT department had four trainers available to provide the live instruction, scheduled to begin in three weeks. The budget was extremely tight.

The Solution

The project tracking application vendor created the curriculum and handed off the materials to the internal IT education team three weeks before the first scheduled pilot. The team had to finish the documentation and coordinate the implementation logistics. Two locations required face-to-face instruction and received the one day training. The rest used live e-learning with teleconferencing for three two-hour sessions. One instructor and one subject-matter expert trained up to eight sites at a time. A site was defined as a one-person office up to a classroom filled with learners using one connection and an LCD projector to view the class presentation. Pre-trained local-site coordinators were used to facilitate exercises at the larger office remote locations. Few people had to travel for any of the sessions.

The Result

The pilot training with 50 students was successful after only three weeks of preparation. Live e-learning was used to reach the additional 850 participants within one month.

VIRTUAL CLASSROOM FEATURES

Core Features

What you need to get by:

- **Whiteboard**—Similar to a flip chart or the blackboard found in the traditional classroom. Someone writes or draws and everyone sees. Variations include instructor control of who can write on the whiteboard, richness of drawing tools, and the saving and printing of the board for later asynchronous use.

- **Graphic Content** (i.e., slides)—One of the most commonly used features. Text or graphical slides are prepared and converted to an image format such as gif or jpg that can be stored and displayed by the virtual classroom system. Most systems provide the ability to use the whiteboard tools to mark-up the graphic content.

- **Synchronized Web Surfing**—This basic capability allows for simultaneous display of a web page on everyone's screen.

- **Application Viewing**—Allows the instructor to show the students a real time view of an application running on the instructor's PC.

- **Instructor Controls**—At a minimum, allows the instructor to control permission of the students to access features of the whiteboard, graphic content, web surfing, or application viewing.

- **Attendance Listing**—Allows the instructor to see a list of all attendees in real-time.

- **Hand Raising**—Without the benefit of the face-to-face classroom environment, it is important to have a procedure that allows the students to alert the instructor that they have a question. The hand raising function allows the student to click on an icon that signals the instructor that they have raised their hand, electronically.

Premium Features

You may want some or all of these to enhance your live e-learning programs:

- **Application Sharing**—Advanced capabilities include the ability of the students to allow viewing of applications on their desktop. Another advanced functionality is the ability to allow others to control the application that someone else is sharing with the class.

- **Text Chat**—This feature enables students to enter messages during the session. You will often see a public chat as well as a provision to exchange private messages with the instructors. In addition to allowing the students to exchange comments, chat can be used by instructors in many other ways:

  - Facilitate student introductions

  - Answer a question asked by the instructor

  - Provide technical support

  - Give a student without an audio connection a way to communicate with the class.

- **Written Question Submission**—Works like text chat, but is specific to students asking questions. Allows more instructor control. Not essential as long as a good text chat is available.

- **Streaming Video**—This feature allows a small video display that can show a head and shoulders web cam shot of the instructor or students. Bandwidth issues can be a problem. Most systems allow a participant to turn off this feature if they have bandwidth limitations.

- **Discussion Board**—An asynchronous component that allows continued threaded discussion between instructors and students at their own pace.

- **Feedback**—Allows students a *one click* input response such as yes/no, applause, laughter, too fast/too slow. Since there are no standards, various vendors provide their own unique sets of feedback features.

- **Polling**—The ability to ask the students a true/false, yes/no, multiple choice, or single answer question. Depending on the system, questions can be prepared in advance or entered in real time.

- **Assessment/Evaluations**—Allows for the incorporation of assessments or evaluations into the system. This eliminates the need to acquire and maintain a separate assessment system for administering, scoring, and tracking results.

- **Asynchronous Access to Content**—Provides structured access to course content.

- **Recording**—Provides the ability to record a session. The most sophisticated vendors provide capabilities that include recording a full movie that captures synchronized audio, slides with real time mark-up/annotation, web safari, and application sharing.

- **Archiving and Playback**—The ability of the system to store a library of recorded sessions with the ability for later viewing.

- **Breakout Rooms**—Gives the instructor the ability to establish a number of smaller classrooms and assign student groups to move into those "breakout rooms" to work independently of the main class. The instructor should also have the ability to move in and out of the various breakout rooms.

- **Assistant or Co-Instructor**—Allows for additional, shared virtual classroom control.

- **Pre-Class Content Loading**—Allows students to load the class content prior to the start of class. This is particularly attractive to students with a slow dial-up connection.

- **Multimedia Content**—Provides for the incorporation of multimedia, i.e., flash, videos, sound into the session. Due to the larger file size of multimedia, pre-loading of content is very desirable, if not necessary.

- **Class Scheduling**—Allows the instructor to reserve space on the virtual classroom system for an upcoming session.

- **Attendance Records**—The ability to store records of session attendance and generate reports from that database.

- **Security**—Features range from basic password protection to encryption.

- **Pre-Class Diagnostic System Check**—This feature allows participants to verify their system configuration prior to the class.

COOKBOOK QUESTION

Which virtual classroom features do you think are necessary for your project?

PURCHASE, HOST, OR PAY-PER-USE?

There are three ways to obtain live e-learning technology. You can purchase the software and install it on your own server. You can also contract with an Application Service Provider (ASP) who will host, maintain, and support the application on their equipment. Finally, you can rent a virtual classroom on a pay-per-use basis.

Consider these factors when deciding which approach to select.

- Capital versus Operating Budget
- *Just testing* live e-learning versus *long-term commitment*
- IT support availability
- Intranet versus Internet
- Content security
- Speed of implementation
- Internal resources
- Firewall implications
- Variable versus Fixed Costs.

THIN OR THICK CLIENT?

Thick Client

- Rich feature sets
- A separate client program
- Up to a 25MB program installation
- CD ROM or slow download installation
- Student installation support required
- IT support and approval required

- No spontaneous attendance

- Program updates require new install with same as above support requirements

- Typically, better IP audio and video.

Thin Client

- Originally, limited feature sets (rapidly gaining ground on thick clients)

- Uses standard web browser

- Less than a 1MB program installation

- Minimal IT involvement

- Typically, a Java applet (temp program installed in your browser) or a plug-in

- Rarely need to support student installation

- Spontaneous attendance possible on a variety of computers versus the thick clients requiring a complex installation process on a specific computer.

COOKBOOK KEY POINT

The best selection is one based on a detailed evaluation of the various vendors' feature sets, pricing, and reputations matched against your own organization's needs.

AUDIO—THE LURE OF IP TELEPHONY

Audio is critical to the success of a live e-learning class. Two-way audio is most desirable for full interaction. However, instructor to student one-way audio can be effective when used in conjunction with text chat input from the students.

Several approaches are available to provide audio for your live e-learning program. The first approach is to use the traditional telephone conference. The second approach is to use the Internet, or a private intranet, to carry the audio on the same medium as we use for viewing web pages. This is called IP audio, short for Internet Protocol audio.

INTEGRATED IP AUDIO

Many vendors provide built-in IP audio capability. The instructor and students communicate over the same connection to the Internet/intranet used for the web conferencing function. An inexpensive multimedia headset-microphone is used in place of a telephone or the built-in PC speakers and microphones. Communication tends to be one person at a time (half-duplex) as compared to regular telephone communications where everyone can speak at the same time. Generally, the instructor has control of the microphone and passes control to a student who has indicated a desire to speak.

Although an IP audio class seems to be more structured and orderly, it lacks the spontaneity of a regular telephone conference that more closely simulates the regular classroom experience.

Additional issues with IP audio stem from the basic technology of IP networks and issues associated with *packet switching* versus *circuit switching*. Sound quality on IP networks can vary more widely from good to very poor than you will find in the regular telephone network. Sometimes IP audio can be very poor if a participant has a slow connection to the network or if there is a lot of traffic on the network at the time of the class. Vendors have developed proprietary technical approaches to provide improved IP audio. Audio quality from vendor to vendor can vary widely, so a careful evaluation of each vendor's audio system, under adverse network conditions, should be conducted before a selection is made.

Most products have an audio tuning wizard that students must use to configure their audio. While the wizard will walk the student through the process when problems are encountered, getting a good audio setup, nonetheless, might require technical support.

Quality audio headsets are a must. Multimedia computers with internal microphones often create a feedback loop, which makes clear audio almost impossible.

Sound cards and internal microphones, especially on older computers, can create audio difficulties. Vendors should be able to provide you with data and suggestions about the level of support required to configure IP audio for students. Be sure to obtain this information from vendors so that you can plan for the appropriate level of technical support.

SEPARATE AUDIO CONFERENCE CALL

This approach will provide the highest quality audio at the highest cost. While the cost of audio conferencing has come down over the last several years, the cost of an audio conference is a significant factor when planning a live e-learning budget.

For planning purposes, an audio conference can range from $.10 to $.30 per minute, per person. Thus, a typical class session of two hours with 25 students can run $300 to $900. This can add up to large expense over a year's time if you hold many classes. For example, one large communications-technology company conducted approximately 30 classes per week. At $.20 per minute, this would amount to a yearly telephone expense of nearly $1 million.

While a figure of $1 million is significant, not all organizations will reach that level. However, telephone conference expense can be significant. If you plan on conducting many virtual classroom sessions over the long term, it would be wise to ask your telecommunications department to evaluate the possibility of purchasing a teleconference bridge which would eliminate the need of paying a teleconference vendor on an on-going basis.

If you select the separate audio conference call option, provide your instructors with telephone headsets. Holding the telephone and using the virtual classroom controls is next to impossible. A speakerphone for the instructor does not provide the necessary quality and can pick-up background noise. Speakerphones for the students are acceptable, however, students should be instructed to put the speakerphone on mute until they wish to speak.

SEPARATE STREAMING IP AUDIO BROADCAST

While this is not a mainstream approach, large lecture classes not requiring a lot of interaction can be accommodated by using a separate IP audio broadcast if your virtual classroom vendor does not provide IP audio capability and telephone conference cost control is a factor.

STREAMING VIDEO

Some virtual classroom vendors offer the ability of the instructor or even all class participants to be able to transmit a small *head and shoulders* live video image of themselves to the other participants. The video image window is supplementary to the primary graphical classroom window and is rarely more than a few inches in size. The idea of the video image is to provide some form of visual connection for participants so that people who are separated by distance and are generally alone during a live e-learning class do not feel isolated.

While video images can add to the increased feeling of virtual presence, it does so at a cost. The costs of implementing streaming video involve the following factors:

- Your choice of virtual classroom vendors will be narrowed down to those who offer video. Consequently, the virtual classroom application may cost quite a bit more than other non-video choices because having video generally falls on the premium side of the value scale.

- In addition to the cost of web video cameras, a PC may have to be upgraded to accommodate the increased load on the computer.

- Support of the web video equipment will add to the total cost of operation.

- Video increases bandwidth requirements and participants with slower dial-up connections may not be able to attend a session with video.

Practical experience in conjunction with several studies has shown that the small *head and shoulders* video does little to improve the learning environment. In fact, many say that the video is distracting during a session where concentration on the audio communication and dynamic graphical image is critical.

An alternative to streaming video is to use static images, perhaps taken by commonly available digital cameras and converted to small jpg images easily transferred via email to the instructor. The instructor can use these images during participant introductions to add that sense of *presence* to a virtual class session.

RECORDING AND ARCHIVING

Same time/different place live e-learning is a great concept that can provide a rich learning experience. The realities of today's business world, however, may preclude everyone from taking advantage of real time events. It is possible that someone will have to miss one or more sessions of a multi-session training program or possibly have a schedule that makes it impossible to attend any live sessions. Should these people be denied the benefits of live e-learning?

Many of today's systems offer the ability to record live e-learning sessions. There is no generally acceptable way to provide this capability. If this capability is important to you (and it should be), a careful evaluation of each vendor's approach to recording, archiving and playback is imperative.

Things to look for:

- Can the instructor initiate and control the recording?
- Is the recording and/or editing functionality integrated into the virtual classroom system or is it a separate program?
- Is the recorded output standards-based or proprietary?
- What speed of network connection does one need to watch the recordings?
- How does the student access the archive?
- Can you secure the archive?
- Can you track and report on the use of the archived recordings?

Selecting the appropriate virtual classroom technology for your specific requirements is a complex, but not impossible task. Hopefully, the guidelines presented in this chapter will help to clarify the alternatives and decision factors.

The trend towards increased availability of renting a virtual classroom on a *pay-per-use* basis will allow you to try before you buy. In fact, a case can be made for the low stress of an on-going rental or contracting with an application service provider versus the more time and labor intensive purchase and maintenance of virtual classroom software, hardware, and Internet circuits.

Virtual classroom features have been presented in two major group-ings, core features and premium features. Premium features help to enhance your live e-learning programs. While this may be true, we emphasize that features alone do not guarantee success with live e-learning. In fact, well designed and delivered course content is the most critical aspect for live e-learning success. To that end, the next chapters will present ideas for designing, developing, and delivering your suc-cessful live e-learning program.

COOKBOOK QUESTION

Who in your organization will need to approve and support your technical implementation of live e-learning?

COOKBOOK SCENARIO

Human Resources Meeting

The Challenge

Faced with travel moratoriums, the vice president of HR for a global financial company had to rethink his group's biannual meeting. The planned topic for discussion was innovation and knowledge sharing. He and his planning team decided to try an online meeting and wanted to make it as interactive as if everyone was physically together.

The Solution

The team carefully designed the three-day event to ensure that group members gained the maximum benefit. Over 60 participants *attended* the live sessions from their offices or homes. They engaged in large group conversation with presentation facilitation via conference calls and small-group breakout sessions via chat rooms. Materials for self-paced learning were sent to each person before the online meeting. After completing an exercise, participants would call teammates to discuss the experience and describe the things they did that they considered innovative.

The Result

People gave positive feedback about meeting online. They effectively shared personal experiences about innovative practices and reconnected with each other. The vice president met the department's requirements of holding the meeting, yet saved substantial travel costs. Supporting materials posted online became a library reference source on the topic of innovation and knowledge sharing that the group continued to use after the meeting.

5

Developing Live E-Learning

Adult learning research tells us that learners will retain knowledge and skills at different rates depending upon the instructional methodology used. When we participate in training, we usually see the following results in learner retention:

- 10 % of what they read

- 20 % of what they hear

- 30 % of what they see

- 50% of what they see and hear

- 75% of what they speak and discuss

- 90% of what they do, practice and apply.

Live e-learning is an interactive instructional method that results in significantly higher rates of learner understanding and retention of training material by combining visual, auditory, and participatory learning strategies. Based on the statistics, live online instruction is an excellent way to retain the strengths of the traditional classroom model and to increase the likelihood your employees will apply their learning more effectively, resulting in a much better return on your time and investment.

ADULT LEARNING PRINCIPLES

Certain adult learning principles are generally accepted as indispensable for successful learning to take place. Attention to the following principles during the design and development of employee e-learning programs helps ensure that content is accepted and applied most effectively. The adult employee learner is someone who:

…has an independent self-concept and is able to direct his or her own learning.
Therefore, develop a friendly and informal learning environment. Help learners diagnose their own training needs and involve them in planning and conducting their own learning. Adult learners can even evaluate their own progress toward learning or performance goals.

…has accumulated a lot of life experiences that become a rich resource for learning.
Therefore, place emphasis on techniques such as field projects or group discussions that tap the experience of the employee. Illustrate new concepts with examples of life experiences drawn from the group. This principle provides the basis for capturing collective knowledge.

…is motivated to learn by a combination of self and public factors.
Therefore, find out what the learners want to know and how knowing the information will help them. Provide various ways for employees to find out the specific information they need, when they need it. Discover *what's in it for me* for each employee, and what work-related rewards might be appropriate.

…wants learning to be closely related to changing social or job roles.
Therefore, adjust the sequence of learning activities to the employees' *need to know*. Perhaps begin a session with a practice try-out

activity rather than a lecture or let them choose what modules to take in which order. Learners can be grouped with peers to share information.

...is problem-centered and interested in immediate application of knowledge.

Therefore, ask what problems the learners are experiencing and what they think should be done to address the issues. Structure the training content and activities to deal with the job-related issues they—and you—feel are important. Instructors can help learners to learn and apply rather than just telling them what they should know.

That last principle leads us to an exciting learning environment that can garner the business goals you expect. While a number of companies may be offering synchronous e-learning, many have not yet begun to utilize the process to its full advantage. Instead of energetic trainers delivering rich interactive content, many are presenting static slides with limited opportunity for the learners to interact with the instructor, their peers, or the content. So how can live web-based instruction parallel, or even exceed, the classroom experience?

COOKBOOK KEY POINT

Do not forget to create a FUN experience!

ACTIVE LEARNING MODELS

The savvy live e-learning instructor takes cues from active learning models. He or she is aware of and practices adult learning concepts and uses real-world outcome models as the roadmap to successful training. Various studies show that the most effective training is that which simulates the actual work environment. Through engaging trainer interaction, quality visuals, peer collaboration, and hands-on practice labs or scenarios, participants can work through real-world problems and processes—just as in the traditional classroom. Your employees are motivated by what will help them solve problems and increase their performance on the job. So your task is to provide them with the appropriate real-world, job-specific learning experiences that meet their needs, and yours.

Action Learning—A real-time learning experience that solves an organizational problem <u>and</u> develops individuals or groups.

Accelerated Learning—An innovative set of interrelated learning experiences that promote faster retention and real-world application of instructional information, leading to more effective business results.

Active Learning—A process that involves putting learners in situations that require them to actively read, speak, listen, think deeply, and write, thus putting the responsibility of organizing what is to be learned in the hands of the learners themselves.

MANAGEMENT ROLE IN E-LEARNING DEVELOPMENT

How can the business manager leverage live e-learning to meet business goals? The answer to that question starts by acknowledging that the business manager has an important role in the training process. He or she has fundamental decisions to make in the development of any training program, be it face-to-face, self-paced, or the live virtual classroom. Let us take a closer look at some of these important strategy decisions.

COOKBOOK KEY POINT

The business manager role is critical in defining the learning outcomes for the learner and the training program.

Developing a live e-learning training program starts with defining, "What are participants able to do when the training program is completed"? If you stay focused on the business outcome—time to market and time to new skills—your training design will most likely be simple and to the point. In our experience, we have found that time invested up front in defining outcomes will have significant payoff in both designing your virtual classroom training program and achieving your business outcomes. As the business manager, your role in defining the learning result is critical. You might delegate responsibility to others to develop the training program, but you must actively work with your team to define the learning outcomes.

The most frequent challenge business managers and trainers face is that there is always more to teach than there is time available. We have found the following three descriptions helpful when aligning e-learning design to business outcomes:

Define *must-knows*—what information or skill training is critical. If employees do not have these must-knows, they will not be able to get the job done.

Define *need-to-knows*—content that is important but at a second level. It might be assigned as pre-class reading, taught in the class, or practiced in "learning exercises" between live virtual class sessions.

Define *like-to-knows*—these are the reference and background informational items. Employees need to know where to get this information but this material is not covered in detail during the training.

To make the point, think about a time when you were trying to learn a new software program. The software came with a manual that you found unusable. You went out, bought a book, and quickly looked up the functional procedures that you needed to know. In a similar way, designing for the live virtual classroom is the same. Stay focused on the outcomes and the functional information people need. Keep it simple.

COOKBOOK QUESTION

What are the business outcomes you want to achieve for your first pilot live virtual classroom training program?

What are the *must-know* skill or knowledge goals that employees must master in order to achieve the business outcome?

COOKBOOK KEY POINT

Make sure that people you assign to develop a virtual classroom-training program clearly define the must-know components required to achieve the outcomes.

You might find the following information helpful. Once you have identified your content, plot it out into the following training delivery modes:

Pre-Class

Identify information that students should review prior to coming to class.

- *Must-know* materials.
- Reading assignments.
- Reference material students should know how to access.

Virtual Classroom

Define the critical content that must be covered.

- Lecture and information.
- Questions to the subject matter expert.
- Trying out new ideas.
- Discussion.
- Case studies.
- Exercises.
- Breakout sessions for practice.
- *Must-know* material to be presented and discussed.
- Exercises and case studies for practice.

Learning Exercises between Classes

- Define practice exercises that employees can do between classes *on the job*.

- Specific time-limited (achievable) goals for *on the job* practice session.

- Study buddies—partner people to encourage discussion about new material being learned.

- Threaded discussion or email exchanges.

COOKBOOK KEY POINT

Decide how the live virtual classroom fits with your department's training strategy—one size does not fit all—to determine what your blended learning strategy will look like.

E-learning can be *blended, synchronous,* and/or *asynchronous*.

Blended learning is usually described as a course that makes use of the traditional classroom experience and the Internet as tools for learning.

Synchronous learning involves the use of live audio (audio conference call or VOIP), a whiteboard for illustrations, and live text chat that enables teachers and students to communicate in real time. The sharing of information between students and the resulting communication closely resembles the collaboration found in traditional face-to-face classes.

Asynchronous learning differs from synchronous because there is a delay in teacher and student interaction. This type of e-learning can be delivered through CD-ROM and web-based self-paced courses, with instructor/student interaction via email, web-based discussion forums, and message boards.

These training delivery strategies do not stand alone. The business manager needs to carefully plan how the use of a virtual classroom will fit into the organization's existing training strategy. For example, using a blended approach, live e-learning might be combined with self-paced learning. A virtual classroom session can mark the starting point for a training program that includes both self-paced and virtual classroom learning. Starting a blended learning initiative with a synchronous real time session can contribute significantly to the success and completion rate of your training program. The virtual classroom:

- Provides a defined starting point that gets scheduled on participant's calendars.

- Creates strong buy-in with the use of a clear learner contract about *what's in it for me.*

- Makes sure everyone is aware of the business outcome and individual payoffs for the learners.

- Creates motivation and commitment for the self-paced learning units.

- Builds in accountability for completion of required self-paced units and provides an opportunity for discussion and questions directly with the subject matter expert.

- Sets the timeline for accountability and completion, and provides an opportunity to celebrate and share what was learned during the course.

COOKBOOK KEY POINT

If you are introducing live e-learning into an existing curriculum, it is advisable to blend it with the current delivery method (classroom, self-paced).

COOKBOOK SCENARIO

Blended Employee Training

The Challenge

Executives of the manufacturing company wanted the firm to begin acting more like the global company it had become. Most locations operated independently, creating a fractured management approach that also affected training. As the executives decided to restructure the company around business processes rather than locale, Human Resources processes like training had to be changed.

The Solution

An HR Management System was implemented, followed by an HR system that offered employees access to career information, training resources, compensation figures, and job opportunities. This system included a standardized, self-paced online training process. However, when first launched the employees were expected to take a course *via* the online learning system to *learn how to use* the online learning system. This did not work as well as they thought it would. The company initiated a blended training program that combined live classroom demonstrations, a published quick reference guide for employees to keep by their computer, and the online training sessions.

The Results

Employees began attending the live sessions to become comfortable with the new system. Once familiar with the changes in training procedures, employee use of the system continuously improved. The major issue of global standardization of course content and delivery was addressed to the satisfaction of the executives.

DEVELOP THE *LEARNING CONTRACT*

One of the major changes for trainers when developing virtual classroom training is to understand the perspective of the learner in the virtual classroom. In a face-to-face classroom there are social norms that hold the class together:

- Learners make the time commitment to attend a class.

- Learners arrive on time—in fact, usually 30 minutes early for coffee and donuts.

- Learners generally stay until the end of the class.

- Learners try to look interested and engaged even if they are multi-tasking or doing other things at their seat.

COOKBOOK KEY POINT

In the virtual classroom, your learner is just one click away from leaving the class and doing something else. If the instruction is not on the mark, learners vote with their behavior and do not participate or do not complete the class.

Implications for designing instructional content for the virtual classroom are:

- You must start with the end in mind. Instruction has to be designed so that the learner understands *right away* what the learning outcomes are, what is expected, and *what benefits they will get from this learning experience.* This becomes the basic learning contract.

- The contract with the learner must be very explicit about the outcomes. What skills will they learn, why are the skills important, what is the business payoff, and what benefits will they gain from this learning experience?

COOKBOOK QUESTION

Designing instructional content starts with a clear contract with the learner. What is the *contract with the learner* for your first live e-learning program?

What are the knowledge or skill outcomes?

Why are they important?

What are the benefits for the learner?

What are the benefits for the company?

COOKBOOK KEY POINT

Try it yourself first! The best way to start learning about the virtual classroom is to take some live virtual classes and get a learner's perspective of the virtual classroom environment.

Experienced synchronous instructors recommend directly experiencing the online environment as both a student and as a trainer in order to effectively design and deliver live content. Trainers say that an understanding of the learner experience is critical to success because, as an instructor, they become aware of what works and what does not. As a part of understanding the learning process and mastering the technology, online student experiences help you—or your instructors—handle the multi-tasking necessary for success. Not only do you need to be familiar with enabling and disabling the application's tools, but you will also be faced with:

- Employing interactive techniques.
- Delivering the content seamlessly.
- Managing discussion and questions.
- Staying on time schedules.
- Overcoming technical issues.
- Managing the overall flow of the class.

CAPTURE THE LEARNER'S ATTENTION

We are comfortable with our educational system. From kindergarten on, we are accustomed to a classroom setting in which the teacher is at the front of the room. In live e-learning, you are the *teacher* but you have no physical *front of the room* to guide your actions and you cannot see the participants. Therefore, make sure you design properly for distance versus classroom-based training.

In the live e-learning environment, you will lose your learner's attention if you solely use the lecture mode. Ask yourself, how long would you stay interested in watching slides on a computer monitor while hearing a voice talk at you on a phone? How long before you begin doing email (since the trainer cannot see you)? Creating an interactive learning experience provides the virtual classroom with a familiar, yet new, atmosphere that is conducive to maximizing results.

INCLUDE THE LEARNER IN YOUR DESIGN PROCESS

To design interactive virtual class sessions, it is helpful to interview a representative group of learners while designing your instructional plan. You must do in-depth research on the perspective of the learner. Work to understand the student perspective of the learning tasks. What are the problems or concerns? What questions are being asked?

Use the following questions when interviewing prospective learners:

- What is most important to them in learning a new skill?

- What tasks are most important? Rank them in order.

- What is your approach to instruction? Lay out a storyboard and validate your approach with a focus group of learners.

- What does the learner think about the instruction? Are their questions about "what is in it for me" clearly answered?

As soon as you have a beta version of the course, plan a rehearsal and try out your instructional approach.

COOKBOOK KEY POINT

Time invested up front involving the learner will increase your chances of achieving the business results required.

You might prepare your course material much quicker without input from the learner. However, when you teach the class and learner evaluations rank the course poorly or performance outcomes are not seen on the job, did you really save time designing the course?

COOKBOOK SCENARIO

Instructor Training

The Challenge

How do you cost effectively provide training for instructors who are making the transition from the traditional classroom to teaching in an online virtual classroom? In 1998, one of the leading web conferencing and virtual classroom software vendors was the first to offer an online training course for corporate trainers to prepare them to conduct live training sessions over the Internet.

The business challenges were:

- The vendor's traditional product support training required a three-day onsite training program.

- Customers implementing the virtual classroom had an urgent need to begin implementation. Scheduling three full work days for training was often a challenge and delayed project start-up.

- Online instructor training was cost and time effective.

The Solution

Making the transition from the classroom to a web-based virtual classroom provided a number of challenges. Corporate trainers had to become familiar with both the student experience as an online learner and new strategies for instructing in an online virtual classroom. The curriculum for a three-day, face-to-face training had to be repurposed for online delivery. Twenty-four hours of face-to-face instruction was converted into a 16-hour online course that included self-study, online virtual classroom sessions, and two-person team learning exercises to be completed between the class sessions. The training outline included:

- An orientation session to introduce the virtual classroom and overview the course content, assignments, schedules, and commitments required to complete the course.

- Self-paced work—Participants had approximately one hour of reading assignments before each of the first three classes. A course manual with the reading assignments was provided.

- Three two-hour virtual class sessions covered both operation of the virtual classroom technology and online instructional strategies. Class content focused on both the student and the instructor roles. Interactive discussion help the participants focus on the personal experience as a student. These personal experiences were translated into important discussion of what an online instructor had to do to facilitate an online learning process.

- At the end of each live class, participants were paired up and assigned learning exercises creating virtual classroom material and practice exercises using the software. Each learning exercise required about 1½ hours of time.

- Following the completion of the third class, participants began preparations for the final exam—creating and delivering their first online virtual class presentation. Participants used existing training material and repurposed the material for the virtual classroom.

- The final virtual class session was a *teach-back* where participants put what they learned into practice!

The Result

The course final exam proved to be an invaluable learning experience for corporate trainers. Having to actually deliver an online class provided an experience that helped them integrate all that they had learned. Corporate trainers came away from the experience with new confidence about their skills and a real understanding of what was required in order to plan and prepare for online instruction. Key concepts they learned were:

- Class plans had to be developed in five-minute intervals. Different from a face-to-face class, instructors had to plan what was happening in much greater detail.

- Lecture in a virtual classroom is deadly. Interactions with students had to be planned at a minimum of every five minutes. Only through interaction did instructors get feedback from students and understand how students were progressing with the learning process.

- They learned a variety of techniques for interactive whiteboard exercises to engage students in discussion, problem solving, and case study discussion.

- And, most importantly, they learned the importance of rehearsals. Rehearsal aided in the preparation process. Good rehearsal enabled the corporate trainers to become comfortable with the technology. Operating the technology became transparent in their online instruction.

STRATEGY DECISIONS—USING THE VIRTUAL CLASSROOM

One size does not fit all training needs. As the business manager, your participation in determining the learning outcomes for a training program is important so that different strategies will be used depending upon what you want employees to learn. This holds true whether you are repurposing an existing training for delivery online or you are developing a new training program.

We end this chapter with a summary of different learning outcomes that can help you choose the most effective applications, formats, and class size for your live e-learning training programs.

Informational Presentations

Outcomes—Communicate business critical information rapidly to large numbers of employees.

Examples—Message from the CEO or strategic business leader, product updates (new product upgrade or version release), market/competitive strategies, strategic business information.

Format—Large virtual classroom sessions. Informational presentation, with an opportunity for limited questions and answers with the presenter.

Numbers—Medium to large groups: 50 to 200 or more participants. Program offered at several different times to reach participants in different time zones—can span to reach global workforces. Program recorded and available for viewing over the web for those who cannot attend.

Seminars

Outcomes—Interactive content presentation, similar to a workshop presentation done in a face-to-face meeting.

Examples—Sales techniques, consulting strategies, value added sales strategies, product updates, new product roll outs, policy and procedure updates, regulatory or safety training.

Format—One session or a series of sessions. Engaging interactive discussions and use of interactive tools separate this type of presentation from an informational presentation.

Numbers—Number of participants: 25 to 50 to allow for discussion, questions and answers, and interactive exercises. Time: scheduled multiple times, offered at times convenient for participants. Option to record the presentation for asynchronous review.

Skill Training

Outcomes—Skill training in a business procedure. Learning requires dynamic interaction between subject matter experts and participants.

Examples—Software training, CRM systems, SAP systems, sales training, new employee orientations.

Format—Series of virtual class sessions combined with pre-class reading assignments and post-class learning exercise assignments.

Numbers—Number of participants: 15 to 30 for highly interactive virtual classroom sessions with use of breakout rooms for case studies and small group exercises.

Blended Learning

Outcomes—Virtual class session, pre or post face-to-face training sessions. Provides support for self-paced learning programs.

Examples—Used to prepare staff in advance of face-to-face meeting or training. Can be used to shorten the number of days required for a face-to-face meeting or used to reinforce learning when employees return to the field. Used to improve completion rate of self-paced learning programs and to provide staff with the opportunity to dialogue with SMEs about course content.

Format—One or two pre-meeting virtual sessions to get everyone prepared for a large meeting. One or two post-session virtual classes can provide coaching for practice of new skills or procedures. Also a three-session model can be used to support self-paced programs: a kick off class at beginning of the course, a mid point class for questions and discussion, and a final class for review and to set a deadline date for course completion.

Numbers—Number of participants: 15 to 30 for small group interactive discussions; can be larger groups if the material is informational in nature

In this chapter, we have focused on business manager decisions that must be considered to develop a successful virtual classroom-training program. As the business manager, you have final responsibility for the business results of your unit. To be certain you achieve these results, use the list of critical decisions presented to make sure you are involved at all the key decision points that will impact your training design.

Your role is to define the business outcome goals. Participating and influencing key decisions will also make it much easier to guide your training department and curriculum design consultants in the production of your training program.

COOKBOOK SCENARIO

Software Application Update

The Challenge

The international program manager for the training arm of a global software company business unit needed to provide a course on software application updates to employees as quickly as possible. In the past, the instructor-led course would have been converted to a videotape and streamed to desktops around the world. This involved hiring a video crew, taping the training, sending the tape to an outside production company to be converted for web streaming, and then installing the final product on the company network.

The Solution

Because it would normally take five to six weeks and cost $21,000 to convert the seven-hour course, the manager turned to the online live virtual classroom that another division of the company was already using. The instructor was recorded teaching the software application over the live e-learning system. Audio, application sharing of the software demos, and the instructor's presentation slides were all a part of the virtual classroom recording. The recording of the virtual classroom presentation was then posted on the company network for self-paced review.

The Result

The course was recorded and streamed to desktops within five to six days, instead of five to six weeks. Edit features were used to localize the materials very quickly for in-country use. Costs were contained to less than $5000, and users around the world received the information more quickly than ever before.

6

Facilitating Live E-Learning

We have talked about designing live e-learning class sessions. Now let us look at what it takes to conduct a class.

If you are like many people experienced with conducting face-to-face workshops or teaching in a regular classroom, you probably have a lot of questions and some concerns about teaching in a virtual classroom. Some of the questions might include:

- How can I be an effective instructor when I cannot see my audience?

- How do I know that my students are engaged in the class?

In the last chapter, we advised you to get a learner's perspective on the virtual classroom environment. Now take a critical look at that live-e-learning experience and answer the following questions. This will help you to evaluate your student experience with the virtual classroom.

- Was it easy to register and were the *coming to class* instructions clear?

- Did you have any technical problems coming to class?

- Was the instructor clear about the goal and purpose of the class?

- Did the instructor keep you engaged? What interactive tools were used?

- How easy was it to participate in class?
- Did you find yourself involved or were you away checking your email?
- What made the seminar engaging?
- What instructional ideas did you pick up?
- What, as a student, did you learn *not to do* in a virtual classroom?

Once you have experienced the virtual classroom from the student perspective, you are ready to begin exploring effective online instructional strategies.

EFFECTIVE LIVE E-LEARNING INSTRUCTION

Why do new instructors find it so difficult to create engaging virtual classroom instruction? It is not that the necessary tools are not available. In fact, they are built right into the software. The key to facilitating learning in the virtual classroom is learning to leverage the interactive tools.

Here are some key points to consider about effective online instruction:

- Online instructors are clear about their instructional goals. They also know that they must be clear about what the *payoff* is for the learner.
- Good instructors engage their participants from the beginning of the class. They actively use the interactive tools in the classroom.
- Instructors intersperse discussions throughout the presentation. Effective online instructors never wait until the end of the class to *open it up for questions*.

- Good instructors never ask *Are there any questions?* and then wait through a long deadly silence on the other end of the line. Instead, they engage participants by calling on individuals by name with engaging open-ended questions to start the dialogue.

- Once a discussion is started, they invite others by name to comment and participate.

- Effective instructors use the hand-raising tool to pull others into the discussion.

- Good instructors learn to scan the interface and monitor the electronic hand raising. They keep the discussion focused and all participants engaged.

COOKBOOK KEY POINT

The eye contact of a live virtual classroom instructor is the dialogue and interaction created with students. Effective live e-learning classroom facilitation might seem easy but, in fact, the points listed above are new skills that must be learned, practiced, and built into your class plan.

COOKBOOK SCENARIO

Distributed Sales Force

The Challenge

With a sales force of 20+ sales representatives distributed over two states, the traditional approach of having them travel to the regional office for monthly meetings was no longer cost effective. Due to budget constraints, the district sales manager was planning to change the monthly sales meeting to quarterly. This change to a less frequent meeting cycle was disturbing to management because rapidly changing product lifecycles and increasing competition necessitated more, not less, team communication. Consequently, management considered conducting weekly telephone conference calls to supplement the quarterly meetings.

The Solution

Instead, management decided to conduct weekly sales meetings over a virtual classroom system in conjunction with a simultaneous telephone conference call. The virtual classroom system was an existing application that had been installed by the training department, and sales meetings were scheduled during open time slots. Because of the frequency and visual collaborative nature of the virtual meetings, the face-to-face meetings were eventually eliminated. Meeting agendas included weekly updates by sales management, a sales showcase presented by a different salesperson each week, and a product presentation by product management that covered new products or existing product updates.

The Results

The original annual cost was $90,000 for 15 of the 22 sales reps that needed to travel to the monthly meetings. The monthly meeting cost of $500 per sales person and was reduced to $72 per person ($18 per sales rep, per weekly meeting) conducted online. The new annual cost was $19,000, a savings of $71,000 per year. Additional soft dollar savings were obtained by eliminating drive or fly time to attend the meetings. This amounted to a productivity return of 1,440 hours not needed for the travel time and equated to having another salesperson in the field, full-time for 36 weeks.

FACILITATING ACTIVE PARTICIPATION

There is a major shift in assumptions about the role of the instructor and the students in a virtual classroom environment. In the traditional face-to-face classroom, the instructor often uses lecture as a primary tool for dispensing information. The instructor has the major responsibility for content delivery. Students play a more passive listening or note-taking role. Instructors and students engage in dialogue when students ask questions.

In the virtual classroom, the instructor's role becomes much more of a learning facilitator. The good instructor has a detailed class plan that includes interactions with the students every five minutes. Students are expected to participate and instructors call on students by name on a random basis. With good class facilitation, the students quickly learn that they might be called on at any moment during the class. The student role shifts from passive to active. Using the polling tools, hand raising, and chat exercises the instructor gets immediate feedback about who is not participating. Simple techniques the instructor can use to facilitate participation include:

- Ask learners to respond *Yes* or *No* by raising their hand or clicking on the Yes/No button.

- Pose a question to the group and ask those who wish to respond to *raise their hand* using the appropriate tool. You might also randomly call on one or two students by name and ask them to type their answer on the whiteboard.

- Ask learners to brainstorm about a specific question or topic by using the chat feature.

- Ask learners to vote by placing a star or symbol next to the item of choice on the whiteboard.

- Create a two column matching exercise. Call on participants to draw lines on the whiteboard matching the items in column A with items in column B.

- Use the polling tool to give learners multiple-choice questions. Then share and discuss the results with the class.

- Quiz learners with multiple-choice and fill-in-the-blank questions. Quizzes are an excellent tool for review, as exercises in applying new knowledge, as well as for more formal testing.

- Finally, use pre-work—a reading assignment, case study—as a tool to stimulate discussion at the beginning of a presentation.

TEAM TEACHING FOR SUCCESS

Before we get to the details of planning a class, let us talk briefly about team teaching in the virtual classroom. It is possible for one instructor to manage and teach in a virtual classroom but chances of delivering a successful class increase dramatically when two people conduct the class. Effective online instruction, especially for newcomers, requires two instructional staff—a subject matter expert or instructor, and a virtual classroom producer.

While the virtual classroom allows you to facilitate a learning process that has many of the advantages of a face-to-face learning experience, it also has some distinct differences. The virtual classroom instructor operates on four different levels simultaneously when conducting a class:

- **Content level**—The presentation of content, learning exercises, and case examples related to the learning outcomes of the class.

- **Planned interactions level**—By design, an instructional plan for a virtual class session will include some planned interaction with students every five minutes.

- **Discussion and facilitation level**—Throughout a class, an instructor will plan points for discussion and dialogue with students. Students also initiate discussion with the instructor or other students when they raise their hand and initiate a question.

- **Classroom technical level**—Throughout a class the instructor will be using the range of interactive virtual classroom tools to support the instructional process and interactions with students. Tools that might be used individually or in combination include whiteboard annotations, chat, hand raising, web tours, application sharing, polls, and quizzes.

COOKBOOK KEY POINT

There is a lot happening in an engaging and interactive virtual classroom session. One instructor can deliver a virtual class, but it can be challenging. The instructor must be well practiced in all the operational features of the virtual classroom. With a two-person instructional team (instructor and producer), responsibilities can be divided and shared.

Instructor Role

- Knowledgeable about content, instructional strategies, and learning outcomes.

- Interpersonal, communication, and organizational skills—lead person on learning facilitation, discussions, learning exercises.

- Facilitates learning experience, encourages learner participation, encourages learners to share and to talk with each other as well as with the instructor.

Producer Role

- Skilled in operations of all technical aspects of conducting a virtual class session.

- Lead person on technical facilitation and a support person for discussions.

- Handles technical problems, monitors hand raising, and operates classroom features (application sharing, web tours, polls, and breakout rooms).

An important management decision is to identify one or two people in your department or in the training department who can play the *producer role.* They will serve as the virtual classroom producers supporting your instructors and subject matter experts. The producer role is a new role in the virtual classroom.

The virtual classroom producer should have the following skills:

- Full knowledge and skills in operating all the features of the virtual classroom: whiteboards, annotation tools, polls, questions and answer sets, chat, application sharing, web tours, breakout rooms, and VOIP audio if used to replace the voice connection using a audio conference call. Producers need to have extensive experience using these features.

- Understanding of how the interactive features of the virtual classroom are used effectively during a presentation.

- Assist the instructor by moderating and/or facilitating discussions. This is a team teaching approach with the subject matter expert focusing on content and the producer focusing on facilitation and virtual classroom operations.

DEVELOPING THE VIRTUAL CLASSROOM LESSON PLAN

In the next section, we are going to take you through how to prepare for a live e-learning class. Our example highlights a typical first class as a company uses the virtual classroom to address time to market or time to skills training. As you follow this example, look for basic information about the detailed operations of the virtual classroom. As we address this typical first application, we will cover basic e-learning training design elements and curriculum development strategies.

Class Preparation Example

PREPARING THE VIRTUAL CLASS SESSION WITH A SME

You have a subject matter expert (SME) with time sensitive information that needs to be communicated to a group of geographically disperse employees. You have confirmed the content, the slides, and the SME. You have all the ingredients with the exception of a virtual classroom plan.

Rather than using a straight lecture format, there are some simple steps your SME can take to quickly adapt the content and presentation to make it much more engaging, interactive, and designed to achieve better learning outcomes. What follows is a set of guidelines for how to work effectively with an SME.

FIRST MEETING WITH THE SME

In this example, your SME has never presented in a virtual classroom. He or she hardly has any idea about how the technology works. Your training department may say, "We will have to train him/her to work in a virtual class setting" or "We should be able to provide the training in four 90 minute online sessions." The reality is your SME is often very busy with a limited amount of time available to prepare the virtual classroom presentation. Your SME often just does not have and will not make the time for "instructor training." What are your options?

The producer can start the virtual classroom orientation by conducting the first meeting with the SME in an online virtual classroom session. Here is a checklist for a typical first planning session:

SME PLANNING SESSION CHECK LIST

Tasks

- Discuss the outcome goal(s) for the session and provide the SME with an orientation to the virtual classroom. Take 10 minutes for the virtual classroom orientation and then go immediately into a review of the outcome goals and content slides.

- Review the slides to determine if the presentation needs to be adapted for the virtual classroom. Identify any handouts or materials that the SME recommends for distribution to participants.

- Plan interaction with participants throughout the presentation.

- Identify edits or slide changes needed. Check for slides with too much text (a good guideline is six words per line, six lines per slides).

- Use graphics for complex concepts.

- Use 30 to 35 slides for a 60 minute presentation.

- Demonstrate how annotations can be used to highlight or emphasize content during the presentation.

- Develop six to eight polling questions.

- Find places in the presentation where the SME can have question and answer discussions with participants. Consider an interactive introduction at the beginning and five minutes of Q&A at about the 15 minute and 35 minute points of the agenda.

- Determine if virtual classroom features like web tours or application sharing will be used. Work out the script for these events—will the producer be responsible for operating the technology under the SME's direction?

- Make your action plan and *to do* lists. You have completed your first work session.

On the basis of this first meeting with the SME, the producer should be able to draft of a time-lined agenda that includes:

1. Agenda items with timelines

2. Script with planned interactions (polls, discussion periods)

3. Interactive classroom features selected for this class

4. Slide revisions list

5. And, a list of handouts and associated materials.

You have just accomplished two steps—you have your content organized now and your SME has been through a painless orientation to the live e-learning classroom. The producer now has a list of the things that need to be done to finalize preparation for the presentation.

Next comes the *production* time when you have to prepare and/or make modifications in the class material. Here is a list of some of the typical and important questions new instructors have when preparing content for the virtual classroom:

- Can you tell me more about how to plan my presentation in five-minute intervals?

- How long should the presentation be?

- What has to be done to convert existing content for the live virtual classroom?

- What do I have to consider when formatting slides for the virtual classroom whiteboard?

- How many slides should a typical presentation contain?

- What about class handouts or reference material?

• What about Student Learning Guides?

PLANNING PRESENTATIONS IN FIVE-MINUTE INTERVALS

One of the most important tasks the instructor and producer have in preparing to teach a virtual class is to develop a detailed class agenda in five-minute intervals. This level and detail of class planning is often new to instructors accustomed to teaching in a face-to-face classroom. The five-minute planning process is a critical tool for online instruction. Without an advanced plan for instructor-student and student-student interactions, the class will fall flat. This might be a hard concept to grasp at first but if you talk to anyone who has been successfully teaching online, the first thing they will tell you is how important it is that you plan out your class in five-minute intervals. An example of a time planning outline is shown on the next page.

LIVE VIRTUAL CLASS TIME PLANNING OUTLINE

Time 0:00

Content

Welcome—intro remarks and first poll question

Process/Interactions

Brief welcome remarks

Poll—experience with today's topic

Slide Reference

#1 Title slide

Poll question 1

Time 0:05

Content

Agenda—graphic with four topic areas

Class ground rules

Process/Interactions

Mini lecture—practice hand-raising for any questions

Slide Reference

2 Agenda

3 Ground rules

All students practice hand raising and lowering

Time 0:10

Content

Student introductions

Student learning goal

Outcome goal for class and expectations

Process/Interactions

Sign in map with name

Chat exercise

Learning goal

Slide Reference

4 Map slide

Intro exercise—in chat, write one personal learning goal you have for today's class

5 outcome goals

Time 0:15

Content

Overview of four topic areas/Intro to topic one

Process/Interactions

Mini lecture

Poll on experience with topic one

Slide Reference

6 Agenda graphic

7 Topic one

Poll question 2

PRESENTATION LENGTH

The rule of thumb is one hour per session. In most workplaces, people schedule in hour intervals. Sixty minutes is also a good length of time to expect people to stay motivated and focused in the learning experience. Here are some time protocols to think about when scheduling the length of a virtual classroom presentation:

- While an hour fits well in most employees' schedules, you can consider 90 minutes for more complex presentations.

- At maximum, do not schedule a presentation to go more than 120 minutes. If you present for two hours, there must be a 10-minute break at the end of the first hour.

PREPARING EXISTING CONTENT FOR THE VIRTUAL CLASSROOM

It is going to be important to sit down with the SME and review the material. Here are some of the key things to review:

- You will need to add a slide with the presenter's picture. A picture is important to help the audience relate to the voice they will be hearing—a simple but important addition.

- If you are doing a 60 minute presentation, that means no more than 45 minutes of content and at least 15 minutes of discussion and/or exercises.

- Do not leave questions and discussion for the end of the class. Work with the SME to find the natural breaks in the content. Build in a 5-minute discussion period at the end of each section of the presentation. You will find that your participants will be much more engaged if they can ask their questions as the presentation progresses.

- Questions and discussion are also very important for the SME. In a virtual classroom you cannot see your participants. Questions and discussion become the *eye contact* or feedback loop for the presenter.

SLIDE FORMATS

Review the slides in advance for format and font size. Here are some basic guidelines:

- Stick with standard Arial or Times Roman fonts.

- Choose a solid slide background color, preferably white or light colored. Dark slide backgrounds are difficult to view on the computer screen for a full hour.

- When preparing slide text, follow these maximum guidelines—six words per line, no more than six lines per slide.

- Some organizations use slides as a way to comprehensively communicate information. Overly wordy slides do not work on the virtual classroom whiteboard. Following the 6x6 rule, use no more than 36 words on a slide. Only use key words and phases. The instructor's verbal comments in class should add value to the information on the slides.

- Use graphics to present key and/or complex concepts. There is truth to the expression—a picture is worth a thousand words!

- Consider developing one graphic slide that represents the five or six key points of the presentation. Insert the graphic at the beginning of the presentation as the agenda slide and then re-insert it at the beginning of each new section of the program. A visual graphic is a good way to help people understand what has been covered and what is still to come in the class.

NUMBER OF SLIDES IN A TYPICAL CLASS

Your presentation should move along quickly—figure no more than two or three minutes per slide. Using this rule of thumb, a 60-minute virtual classroom presentation should have no more than 30 to 35 slides.

CLASS HANDOUTS AND REFERENCE MATERIALS

Determine if there is material you want to share with the audience before or after the class. You can distribute all sorts of material pre or post session but keep in mind that most people are overloaded with information. A good question to ask is, "If participants have time to read just one item before the presentation, what should it be"?

STUDENT LEARNING GUIDES

One simple and effective way to make a student learning guide is to distribute the instructor's slides to the students in advance of the class. Instruct students to print out a copy of the slides in "handout" format, 3 slides to the page. This makes a simple but effective study guide for the class session. Since the students have a copy of each slide, they do not need to take notes on slide content. The note-taking area of the handout is a great place for students to capture discussion notes.

SECOND MEETING WITH THE SME

This second meeting with the SME is a full dress rehearsal for the virtual classroom session.

REHEARSAL TASKS CHECK LIST

- Do a dress rehearsal of the class with a live audience—co-workers, friends, or a small sample of the target audience.

- Ask your SME to attend the rehearsal from the office and computer that will be used during the class. This way you will be able to do a technical test of the audio and virtual classroom setup. If your SME is traveling, be sure that a pre-class technical check is scheduled from the location to be used on the day of the class.

- Coordinate the roles of the producer and the SME. The producer role might include hosting the start of the program and facilitating the Q&A discussion periods while the SME focuses on the content and case study discussions.

- The SME and the producer can work out tasks like annotating on slides—some SMEs prefer to stay focused on their presentation and are comfortable with the producer adding annotations. Others really like the annotation feature and will incorporate its use into their presentation style.

- The producer will operate any special features like application sharing, web tours, or breakout rooms. These features need to be rehearsed and practiced so the SME will know what to expect during the live e-learning class.

- Be prepared and expect to make some modifications to your slides and the class plan following the rehearsal. It never fails—some things are not seen until you actually do the rehearsal.

MEETING ONLINE BEFORE THE PRESENTATION

Finally, the SME and the producer need to meet online at least 30 minutes before the actual presentation to coordinate last minute details on the presentation, and make sure that the virtual classroom technology is working as expected.

PREPARATION ON THE DAY OF CLASS

1. Clear your desk—Put away files, folders, and papers you do not need.

2. Before you teach, reboot your computer and have open only the programs and/or documents you will need during the class. Close your email and calendar program. You do not want distractions from calendar or email pop up windows during your class. Closing unnecessary programs frees up computer RAM assuring that your computer will perform at its best.

3. Presenters must have quality headsets and microphones. If you will be using a conference call, this is much preferred over a speakerphone. A headset will give you the best audio quality, and your voice level will stay the same even as you turn your head to reach for a piece of paper. Speakerphones, unless high quality, can make you sound like you are booming or in an echo room. If using VOIP, you must have a headset that connects to the sound card of your computer. Be sure to do an audio sound check at the beginning of the 30-minute pre-class check-in.

4. Print out your slides in advance, three or six to a page, and have the printout on your desk. A paper copy of the slides is very valuable if you want to look forward or check back during

your presentation. A paper copy of your slides is also a critical part of your disaster planning.

5. Your class plan—A chart breaking down in five minute intervals how you are covering your content and indicating when and where you will build in interaction during the class.

6. A large glass of water.

7. A note pad—Use this to make notes as the class progresses. One tip you might consider is to create your own *virtual seating chart* as participants introduce themselves. Make notes about each student. Put a check by participants' names as they contribute during the class. A quick scan of your list can help you quickly see whom you have called on and who has not yet had a chance to participate in the discussion.

8. Finally, some instructors find it helpful to have a second computer set up in their office, signed into the class as a student. This gives the instructor a chance to see exactly what the students are seeing.

LIMITED PREPARATION TIME—CONTINGENCY PLANS

With the speed of business today, there will be times when you are faced with a situation where your SME either does not have the time or will not make the time to prepare for a virtual class session. While we do not like to admit it, there will be times when you are faced with these circumstances. In this second example, let us look at things a producer can do to prepare for the class and protect the SME from total embarrassment and fumbling in front of peers or customers.

Here is a list of contingency plan action steps:

- Have a phone conversation with the SME at least two weeks in advance to confirm the schedule for the presentation and request a copy of any slides and materials. Try to schedule a rehearsal but, if that fails, get the SME's commitment to join you in the virtual class session at least one hour prior to the class to go over a basic orientation to the virtual classroom environment.

- Confirm where the SME will be on the day of the class and work with a technical assistant at that location to ensure the SME's audio and computer are properly configured and can successfully connect with the virtual classroom. Make no assumptions here. Do a full test connection to the classroom from the computer the SME will be using.

- Review the SME's slides. Check the formatting of the slides. Add title slides and a slide with a picture of the SME, if available.

- Annotations during the presentation—without any orientation to the virtual classroom you cannot expect the SME to operate any of the classroom annotation features. As the producer, you will have to familiarize yourself with the content and be prepared to do slide annotations for the SME as he or she goes through the presentation.

- Define your producer role with the SME and be in charge of the introduction, managing questions and closing the presentation. Explain to the SME how participants will be able to ask questions by raising their hands or submitting questions in the chat.

- Determine if there are one or two points in the presentation where you could insert a five-minute question and answer section into the presentation. Be prepared to suggest these discussion points with the SME. Indicate that, as the producer, you will manage and facilitate the discussion, recognize participants who have raised their hand or are sharing questions that have come in through the chat. This minimum effort for participant interaction with the SME will be an important addition and will get a better result than waiting until the end of the presentation for questions.

- During the hour before the presentation, provide the SME with an orientation to the virtual environment. Try to make him or her as comfortable as possible. Focus on demonstrating only the classroom features that will be used for the class, nothing more.

- Finally, manage your expectations. Produce the best class you can given the circumstances. Know that once the SME has had an experience with a virtual classroom presentation, he or she will better understand the importance of a rehearsal and advance planning. You discuss this when you debrief the SME after the class.

COOKBOOK SCENARIO

Contract Administrator Training

The Challenge

A large telecommunications company needed to quickly and continuously train 50 North American contract administrators on new contracts documents. Typically one contract administrator supported a large geographical district, so sending each to the corporate office would create a significant impact to sales support in addition to the training cost. With new contracts, the legal department wanted to quickly improve the proficiencies of contract administrators. Given the distributed nature of the sales offices as well as a lean HQ legal staff, conducting an extensive road show to train audiences of one was expensive and impractical. Voice conference calls had been used previously, but the lack of visuals frustrated the trainer as well as the contract administrators because the group was constantly waiting for someone to find the right section of the new contracts.

The Solution

The legal department explored using video conferencing but was not satisfied with its ability to show details of a document. Also, video conferencing equipment was not readily available or easy to operate. Finally, the legal team turned to document conferencing to augment a voice conference call. In addition to sharing a presentation of the new contracts and associated processes, the document conferencing tool allowed the lead contract administrators to demonstrate the new contract documents effectively. They could receive the training using standard company communications links—telephone and modem/LAN connections from anywhere around the country.

The Results

The lead trainer repeated the training several times over two days to accommodate different time zones and schedule preferences of 50 contract administrators. With data conferencing, logistics for the class were greatly reduced by eliminating the need to distribute complete sets of the presentation and new contracts prior to the training. The training was so effective that the regional contract administrators duplicated the training sessions for the sales managers.

CREATING INTERACTIVE LIVE E-LEARNING CLASSES

In this section, we will look at the variety of techniques you can use to facilitate interaction and make instruction compelling.

Our instructional goal is always to help learners master new information, new skills, or new ways of thinking that will improve their bottom line job performance. Lecture is the traditional tool that has been used to transfer information. By and large, however, it is a very poor instructional approach for the virtual classroom.

Remember that learners will retain:

- 10 % of what they read.

- 20 % of what they hear.

- 30 % of what they see.

- 50% of what they see and hear.

- 75% of what they speak and talk about.

- 85 to 90% of what they do and practice.

COOKBOOK KEY POINT

Learners will retain 75% of what they talk about and 85 to 90% of what they do and practice. You want your virtual classroom to focus on instructional strategies that engage your audience—get participants talking and guide them toward immediate practice on the job.

In this next section, we will take an in-depth look at how each of the virtual classroom features might be used in your class plan. We will examine the major virtual classroom features found in most live e-learning software including:

- Whiteboard

- Polling

- Chat

- Facilitating discussion in virtual classrooms and breakout rooms

- Application Sharing

- Web Tours.

Finally, we will explore briefly pre- and post-class assignments and look at how they can contribute to your classroom discussion.

WHITEBOARD

This is the virtual classroom tool that displays your slides. From the previous chapter you already know:

- Wording should be simple and capture key points.

- Graphics are an important tool for presenting complex ideas.

- Use slides to present mini lectures reviewing information students were asked to read before class or for presenting new information. Keep your lecture material brief and to the point.

- Mini lectures should run no more than five to seven minutes.

- Lecture is supported with the annotation tools to highlight key points. Check marks, highlighting, boxes and circles, and underlining will add a dynamic visual emphasis and help your participants follow you through the material.

BUILDING INTERACTIVE WHITEBOARD SLIDES

Instead of including all the information on a slide and talking to it during your presentation, prepare a slide with only part of the information and leave some blank spaces. You can call on a student and ask them to help you complete the slide. You can use the annotation tool to type in the student's response or ask the student to type in the information. Let your content provide the opportunities for developing interaction. You can have students complete a flow chart or network drawing, write formulas, or list key points.

WHITEBOARD AS A FLIP CHART

When you want to have a five-minute discussion, for example, use the whiteboard for note taking. Include one or two blank slides in your presentation at the point where the discussion will occur. They can be used for taking notes just like you would use a flip chart to summarize discussion points in a face-to-face classroom.

WHITEBOARD FOR CASE DISCUSSION

Assume for a moment that you are working with a group of sales executives discussing a case study on qualifying a new prospective customer. There are four key points in your *qualifying model.* A slide is used to introduce a case study example. The next slide should have room for the discussion notes on the four points of your qualifying model. As you facilitate the case discussion, call on one sales executive to discuss the first point. Quickly ask three additional sales executives to each take one of the other three areas and fill in key information using the typing tool. When you are finished with the first point, move to point two and engage that sales executive in a discussion of what was typed on the whiteboard. Continue until all four points of the qualifying model are discussed. You now have four people engaged in the case study discussion and the whole class on their toes because they do not know who you will call on next!

WHITEBOARD FOR ROLE PLAY AND LEARNING EXERCISES

A role-playing exercise can be a powerful tool. The secret to success is to have the detail of the roles worked out and the situation well defined beforehand.

Here is an example of a role-play phone conversation between a sales executive and a prospective customer. The objective is to present the value proposition and get the appointment for a face-to-face meeting with the customer. Pick one person to play the sales executive and another person to play the customer. The role play goes no more than five minutes. Following the role play, debrief the customer, debrief the sales executive and then call on others in the class for their comments and observations. Use the whiteboard to capture key points.

POLLING, YES/NO, AND HAND RAISING

With the polling tools in the virtual classroom, you have many ways to frequently engage your participants.

POLL BEFORE PRESENTING INFORMATION

Rather than just lecture learners in a passive-receptive mode, use the polling tool to engage them frequently. A good approach is to do a poll before you provide the expert information. For example, you might want to prepare in advance a polling question like "Our competitor's market share increased/decreased +5, +3, +1, -1, -3, or -5 percent during the last quarter"? Use the poll to engage participants in the content before you provide the facts. Conduct the poll and then share the results so that the entire class can see the poll results. If they were on the mark they will feel good. If they missed the mark, you now have them listening closely to your information to discover why their answer was not correct.

You can also use the Yes/No or hand raising tools for quick polls. This also gives the instructor quick feedback on who is not paying attention or multi-tasking. You might want to call on someone who did not respond to the poll just to make sure they are with the class. You only have to do this a couple of times and everyone learns that the class is interactive and they have to stay attentive.

POLLS FOR DEBATE AND DISCUSSION

A good debate question can add a lot of energy to a discussion. Have you ever been in a workshop where the leader said, "Ok, those who agree with opinion A go to the left side of the room and those who agree with opinion B go to the right side of the room and those who cannot make up their mind go to the back of the room!" Ask a question about your content that is appropriate for debate and use the polling or hand raising tool to ask people to select which side of an issue they are on. Then call on people from each side, facilitating a discussion about the pros and cons of the question.

CHAT

In online classes, chat can be used as a way for students to submit questions to the instructor during the class. This is one basic use of chat and something the producer should be monitoring throughout the class, passing questions on to the instructor at the appropriate times.

Chat can also be used to get everyone participating in an exercise. Design a question related to your content. Assign all class participants to type their comments in the chat area for three minutes. Your chat will explode with student comments.

The instructor and the producer scan the comments to find key observations and common themes. Return to the whiteboard to discuss the themes and key comments that came up in the exercise. This is a good technique for engaging everyone and quickly getting input from all the participants in a short amount of time. Most virtual classroom software allows you to save the chat for later use.

FACILITATING DISCUSSION IN THE VIRTUAL CLASSROOM

Have you ever paused and then asked for questions during a class? Do that in a virtual class session and you might be faced with a long period of silence. Be prepared to start any question or discussion period by

having a good, open-ended question and calling on a specific participant. Be random with who you direct the question to. Use a note pad
with your virtual seating chart and place a mark each time a student
participates in the discussion. This can be an invaluable tool to help
you decide who to call on next.

COOKBOOK KEY POINT

Gone forever is the age-old question, "Are there any questions"?

Your questions and participants' responses are your **eye contact** with
the class. Listen well because this is your opportunity to get feedback
on how participants are dealing with your subject matter. Are they getting it? Are they missing the point? You will find out by challenging
them in a well-facilitated discussion. When participants respond to
being called upon, briefly engage them in the discussion, thank them
for their comments, and then call on someone else to get a second
opinion on the discussion question. By this point, you should be off
into a lively discussion. Let others know to raise their hand if they want
to join in the discussion. This is one of the most rewarding parts of the
live virtual classroom.

Here are a couple of key points for good facilitation:

- Always thank participants for their comments, even if you do
  not agree with them. If you are judgmental or have to *always be
  right*, you will quickly discourage participation.

- Think out in advance the goal of each discussion period. What
  do you want to accomplish? Help participants explore the topic
  using open ended questions. Be patient as participants struggle
  and explore a new idea—do not take them off the hook too
  quickly.

- Be assertive when someone tries to move the discussion off track. You might try:

  "John, that is a valid point but off the subject up for discussion now." Gently call on another student, restating the discussion question.

  Or, "John, that is an important point but off the point of this discussion. Can you save that until the end of class and let's address it in our final discussion period."

  Or you might invite John to contact you outside of class to discuss the question.

- Try not to prematurely end a discussion. Use your best judgment in deciding when it is time to summarize the discussion, and claim a *teaching moment* relating the discussion to the course outcome goals.

- Keep to your time agenda. When you have come to the end of the allotted discussion time—call time, summarize, and move on with your instructional plan.

DISCUSSION USING BREAKOUT ROOMS

There will be times when your class plan calls for participants to go to breakout rooms to work in small groups on a case study or learning exercise. Be sure that you and the producer are well coordinated on moving the class into breakout rooms. Some virtual classroom products use VOIP for audio in breakout rooms. You also can use the breakout room feature with conference call audio if you schedule the breakout rooms in advance. The conference call operator must have detailed instructions on how the groups will be broken out during the breakout sessions.

For successful breakout sessions:

- Have clear instructions about the exercise.

- Define what is expected.

- Define time boundaries.

- Define what each group's final product or outcome is.

- Each breakout session has a session leader who can act as the facilitator and is familiar with the whiteboard and interactive features.

Just like a breakout exercise in a face-to-face class, participants spend time in small groups working on an activity and reporting back to the full class. Be sure you have planned in detail with the producer how to conduct the recap when everyone returns to the large class. Good planning and careful monitoring of time are keys to success for breakout room learning exercises.

APPLICATION SHARING

Application sharing allows the instructor to open and share an application running on the computer with all the participants in the virtual class. Know exactly what you want to share in the class and that you have tested out the application in rehearsal. For training on software, database, and engineering drawing tools, this is a powerful instructional tool. Since application sharing can have an impact on bandwidth, test it out in rehearsal. Set up a test computer to access this process at the slowest connection speed expected during the class to see how the application sharing performs.

Again, you will want to plan for interactions. Let us say that you are demonstrating a database program. After the initial introduction, call on participants and ask them to formulate a search question for the database. Enter data as they direct and then execute the search. Everyone will see the results. If the application sharing permits, you can also pass the controls to a student and have them directly operate the program with everyone viewing the results.

When using application sharing to teach software functionality, keep in mind that demonstration is only part of the learning process. Students will learn some things by watching, but they will learn more when they actually get to do it *hands-on.*

Following an application sharing demonstration, an effective instructional strategy is to have students minimize the virtual classroom and open up their local copy of the software on their computer. The instructor guides students through a hands-on exercise using only the audio conference, thus giving each person experience with their first operation of the software. At the end of the class, you might want to consider assigning learning exercises the students can practice on the job before the next class.

WEB TOURS

The final tool in the virtual classroom is the function that takes your class on a web tour. For example, you can take the class as a group to specific pages of the company website to learn where to get resource information. The class can tour competitor websites to evaluate competitive offerings. Some virtual classroom web touring systems also permit the instructor to annotate and highlight items on the web page being viewed. Participants bookmark sites during the tour to visit after class. Plan in advance your discussion questions so that you can facilitate an ongoing discussion with different students about the sites being visited during the tour. And, of course, do not forget to practice the web tour during your rehearsal.

COOKBOOK QUESTION

How will you plan engaging interactivity for your first virtual classroom program? Select two or three of the techniques covered in this section to incorporate into your class plan. Plan to practice the techniques during your rehearsal.

EFFECTIVE VOICE IN ONLINE COMMUNICATION

A variety of strategies can help make your presentation engaging. Some instructors use a team teaching approach, pairing with the producer or another instructor. Similar to a radio show, you can use more than one voice to provide a change of pace and variations in presenter voice and style. The following information provides some good tips on the use of your voice in a virtual classroom. This information is used with the permission of Paul Marr, Paul Marr Productions.

Passion for the topic
If we are not genuinely excited about our topic, participants will not be either. This is more important than everything else combined.

Enthusiasm
We need to *step it up* two notches above one-on-one conversation.

Dynamics
Voice pitch, speed, and tone must vary. For example, key points need to be emphasized. Or, as we get excited about a point our pitch can rise. Or as we are listing things, we can increase our pace in dramatic fashion. As we make our next point and our voice slows back down to our comfortable pacing, the previous point automatically stands out.

Pauses
Especially when we cannot see our participants, our tendency is to fill the airwaves continuously. But we must leave space for the learner to absorb information. Plus, a well-placed pause following a dramatic point makes the point that much stronger.

Preparation
Our credibility is much more in question when we are not in the same room with the learner. That is augmented when there is no video. If we are not extremely well prepared, we are likely to stam-

mer, stop and start, and seem disjointed which will cause the learner to tune out.

Vocal Surprises

They catch the learner off guard and re-focus them. For instance, if you momentarily slip into falsetto to imitate a woman, learners are curious.

Smile

It cannot be seen, but it can be felt. A smile is contagious.

Emphasize the positives

Without consciously thinking about it, we often send positive or negative messages to our learners. Our voice is the hero or the culprit. If we consciously focus on emphasizing the positive, our message will be better received.

Comfortable range

We should find and use our natural, *most comfortable* vocal range. For instance, as we get excited our voice pitch tends to rise, which is more difficult to listen to and strains our voice. It is effective when used sparingly, but annoying when used consistently.

Posture

How and where we sit/stand affects our voice. Standing is ideal for giving our voice the ultimate oomph it needs. But if we are seated, we need to sit up straight in the chair, preferably perched on the edge of the chair, feet flat on the floor, not touching the chair back.

Speak Distinctly

No one wants to listen to a mush-mouth, especially when they cannot see the mush-mouth! Be careful about touching your face while speaking. Many people have a habit of touching their face or holding their chin with their hand while sitting at a desk or in a phone conversation. These mannerisms will affect the sound of your voice.

COOKBOOK KEY POINT

In the virtual classroom, the instructor must rely on his/her voice to communicate effectively.

Use a top quality headset and microphone when teaching using either an audio conference call or VOIP. Using a speakerphone when conducting an audio conference call just does not generate the quality needed for a professional presentation. A headset, however, will assure that the quality of your voice remains the same even if you turn to the side to access a reference document. The headset also keeps your hands free to access your mouse and keyboard for annotations and operation of the virtual classroom.

LEARNING EXERCISES

Assigned learning exercises between virtual class sessions can support the learning process by encouraging participants to practice on the job between virtual class sessions.

COOKBOOK KEY POINT

Live e-learning is creating a revolution in the training field. Well-designed learning exercises enable participants to practice new skills on the job and return to the next class to report on their practice experiences.

Access to the instructor while new skills are being practiced can significantly shorten the learning curve and achievement of the final learning outcomes. The objective is to design exercises that encourage immediate use of new skills on the job. Consider two key points when designing learning exercises:

- Design the learning exercises so that they are achievable. Do not make the assignment too complex. Clearly define the time required and the expectation for the assignment. Hold students accountable for completing the assignment before the next class.

- Use the *study buddy* approach rather than individual assignments. Pair up participants and assign them to work together or, at a minimum, talk with each other by phone about the results of their practice assignment. Keep in mind that participants will remember and integrate new information or skills when they talk about and practice those skills.

Be sure to plan time in the next class for discussion of the learning exercises. Participants will often bring great comments, ideas, and questions to the next class once they have had an opportunity to practice on the job.

BRINGING STUDENTS TO CLASS FOR THE FIRST TIME

The virtual classroom saves time and money associated with travel. It also saves the cost of face-to-face meeting rooms and/or classrooms. The virtual classroom software is, in fact, your virtual classroom. There will be costs associated with providing students the needed technical support for issues they might encounter coming to class.

Here are some points to consider:

- Set up procedures and give clear directions to students on what they must do to prepare to come to their first virtual class session.

- Many virtual classroom vendors include *self-test* processes a first time user can use to test browsers, Internet connections, and the operation of the virtual classroom. Encouraging students to conduct the self-test can avoid many technical difficulties.

- If a student encounters technical difficulties, be sure to provide a phone number for technical support or a help desk that can help them resolve the issues

- Some organizations require that *first time* students attend a virtual classroom orientation session. In addition to learning basic information about the course, the orientation provides the opportunity to "test connections" and uncover potential technical issues students might encounter.

- If you do not conduct orientation classes, be prepared to allow time in your first session for some of these coming-to-class issues. It is also a good idea to have students log on ten minutes in advance of the class start time.

Every instructor should be familiar with the available technical support resources. Once a virtual classroom session has started, the instructor's full attention must stay focused on the teaching. An instructor cannot stop the class to handle one student's technical problems. If a student encounters technical problems during the class, the instructor must have a technical support phone number to give to the student. The student is responsible for contacting technical support and return to class when the technical issue is resolved.

OFFICE HOURS WITH THE SME OR INSTRUCTOR

Best practice live e-learning courses include instructor or SME office hours. Make sure you clarify how the SME or instructor will be available between classes for student questions and learning support. Here are a number of ways instructors and SMEs can be available to students:

- Email support

- Instructor answering questions in threaded discussion

- Phone appointments with students

- Office hours using the virtual classroom—students can attend a scheduled office hour session. The instructor is available at a specific time for any students who choose to attend. This can be a very efficient way to provide support to learners.

PLANNING FOR THE UNEXPECTED

Technology does have its challenges. Even though virtual classroom software is now well developed, computer and Internet technology can at times throw you an un-anticipated curve. It is imperative that you take some time to prepare yourself for the eventuality that something might go wrong.

TECHNICAL CHALLENGES

You might face five general types of technical challenges while conducting a class:

Browser freezes up
On a rare occasion your browser might freeze, requiring you to close your browser and then reopen the browser to rejoin the class. Work out roles between the producer and instructor if this would happen and then actually practice the event.

Computer crash or power outage
If you encounter major computer problems during a class, you probably will not recover during the class. This could be either a problem with your computer or a power outage. These are situations when it is critical that the instructor has a printed copy of the slides and the class plan at hand. If you are using a conference call for the audio, you can continue to teach from your slides while the producer operates the virtual classroom and tells you what is happening (poll results, who is raising their hand). It is a less than perfect way to teach, but you can conduct the class.

Loss of your Internet connection

If you lose your Internet connection due to technical difficulties, apply the same strategy as when your computer crashes. Use the audio conference to complete what you can, and work with the class to schedule the next session.

Conference Call and VOIP audio problems

Conference call audio problems include audio noise from participant sites. Make sure participants know how to use the conference call mute features to control local site noise. Also make sure participants understand the difference between the mute function and the hold button. Many companies have music-on-hold which can be very distracting during an online session. For interactive classes, the audio bridge should be in open, fully interactive mode. If you are conducting large informational sessions with more than 25 participants, consider using of an operator-assisted conference call with the instructor setup in a 'broadcast mode' along with an operator-assisted 'question queue' for discussion periods. VOIP audio requires that each student use the product's tuning wizard to set up the audio. Some students wait until the last minute only to discover that they have difficulty with their audio. Feedback problems can disrupt the entire class or a participant's ability to participate in VOIP discussions. Have a plan and technical support available to address these concerns.

Instructor teaching from a new computer on the day of class

This is a real sleeper technical problem. Always make sure that instructors and SMEs teach from the same computers on which they rehearsed. If an instructor is traveling and will be using someone else's computer for a class, always do a test session from that computer. You do not want to discover technical problems five minutes before a class starts.

This chapter provided you with some basics for successful online instruction. We focused on several initial issues that a new virtual classroom instructor will encounter. If you use the guidelines provided here, you can significantly improve the implementation of your first online classes. We have outlined a number of class planning and instructional strategies that, if employed, can significantly improve your content delivery, student interactivity, and the achievement of your outcome goals.

COOKBOOK SCENARIO

Real Estate Broker Training

The Challenge

This large real estate firm had traditionally relied on classroom training combined with videos and CD-ROMs to train their remote and off-shore brokers who specialized in high-end properties. The brokers had to travel to mainland U. S. training sites, taking time away from their clients and incurring hefty travel expenses.

The Solution

The firm conducted a series of online seminars to train the brokers on new company policies and high-end sales methods.

The Result

Brokers living and working in remote locations no longer had to travel extensively. They interacted dynamically with the instructor and communicated with their peers to share successful sales techniques. The brokers are much happier, and the firm substantially improved the speed at which information is now delivered to specialized agents around the world.

7

Supporting Live E-Learning

SOME THOUGHTS ABOUT LEARNING AT YOUR DESK

Learning at the worksite is a cultural change for many employees. Learners are faced with new challenges when attending a class from their desk. Here are some strategies that early adapters to desktop learning have found useful. These ideas may help guide you as you begin to develop learning support strategies.

In our experience working with companies implementing live e-learning, we have seen a direct correlation between front line supervisor support and learning outcomes for employees attending desktop virtual classes. If the front line supervisor is supportive, he or she will do what it takes to make sure that their employees get the support needed to be successful and achieve the business outcomes.

DISTRACTIONS DURING THE VIRTUAL CLASS SESSION

Build a culture that takes online learning as seriously as classroom training. In most offices, when a co-worker sees you sitting at your desk, it means that you are available for a question or conversation. It is customary for fellow employees to knock quickly on the door, walk into your office or workstation, and ask a question. This is a real challenge to the learner who is focused on participating in a 60 or 90-minute online class.

Here are examples of how some companies address the issue of interruptions:

- Supervisors circulate informational memos to all employees in the office explaining the new virtual classroom program, the times, the participants, and the dates. Co-workers are requested not to interrupt fellow employees during these training times. These memos also serve as a tool to introduce all employees to this new training resource.

- However, a memo is not enough to change behaviors. Some companies distribute "Do not disturb—e-learning going on" signs that participants can post on the entrance to their cubicles or offices. Other organizations go a step further and distribute yellow tape (similar to police tape) that employees tape across the doorway to their office or cubicle during a class, making it very clear that they are not available.

- When employees attend a class from their office cubicles, the interruption challenge goes both ways. If an employee is using a speakerphone for class participation, co-workers in adjoining workstation also listen to the class. The best solution here is to make sure that employees have telephone headsets.

- In cases where employees do not work at a desk, you will need to schedule offices or conference rooms for virtual classroom sessions. Each employee will need a computer and a phone.

Even with these learner supports, the working environment in some offices generates distractions that are hard to overcome. Cost and time savings associated with live e-learning have encouraged some companies to identify and assign specific offices or other locations that can be used by employees during virtual classroom training sessions. Using flextime procedures, some organizations permit employees to work from home on days when they attend virtual classroom training sessions.

There are distractions that employees control directly. Here are some environmental control tasks that learners are responsible for:

- Turn off e-mail and instant messaging during an online session. The instructor can encourage participants to close desktop applications but the employee makes the final decision. Motivated participants will naturally minimize these distractions.

- Answering phone calls during a virtual class session is a guaranteed interruption. It will also challenge the entire class if your office phone system has music-on-hold.

Employees are motivated to control these distractions when they understand and are invested in the training outcomes. *Office culture* issues need to be addressed in order to support employee learning from their desks.

REGISTRATION AND TRACKING

A majority of the virtual classroom products on the market today include a system for scheduling classes, managing student registration, tracking attendance, and testing results. How this system works will depend upon the specific product your organization selects. Many virtual classroom products have their own stand-alone registration system; others are integrated with a Learning Management System (LMS) or linked to the HR system that your company uses for tracking employee-learning programs. When setting up your virtual classroom program, you will need to plan for the registration and tracking requirements of your program. You should consider:

- Course registration procedures.

- Tracking requirements for attendance, course exams, and participant evaluations.

- Material distribution procedures.

- Self-checks of connections, browsers, plug-ins, and software installation.

- Procedures and instructions for coming to class for the first time.

- Orientation to the virtual classroom and tips for learning online.

Good pre-planning enables you to keep the technology transparent to employees so that they focus on learning and applying the content rather than on the tools used to deliver that content.

Commitment to successful implementation means commitment to the detailed preparation required to support you program. You will need a team of people focused and committed to successful achievement, and a vehicle for employee feedback and program evaluation for continuous program improvement.

COOKBOOK SCENARIO

Learning Management System

The Challenge

This multi-product international company needed to introduce their training coordinators, located worldwide, to the new Learning Management System (LMS). The LMS would be used to manage the enterprise-wide delivery and tracking of training programs. LMS-qualified trainers were scheduled for U.S. and European city tours when significant travel budget cuts were implemented. A less expensive way of delivering the training and developing the communities of practice had to be found.

The Solution

The Training Department decided that a blend of self-paced and live online learning would build the interaction between the LMS trainers and company training coordinators required to create the community of practice. Self-paced materials were used between online sessions for learners to review qualification exam content and test their skills using the new LMS software. The live sessions built relationships and set a positive tone for the global communications.

The Result

Learners worldwide were informed about the training and participated in scheduled online sessions, saving substantial travel costs. The class spanned a two-week period but time away from the job amounted to only hours. Out of the 30 people who completed the course, eight attempted the qualification exam with five passing at 80% or higher. Non-native English speakers had time to review and digest content at their own pace. The materials now reside on the LMS for use by future new training coordinators.

Successful live e-learning involves managers, learners, designers, and instructors who are flexible, adaptable, and willing to take risks. The technology is only a tool that creates the interactive learning environment. Marketing and setting expectations are crucial to creating a learning environment for your employees.

COOKBOOK KEY POINT

Your students do not care about the internal operations of the technology. Provide guidelines that will help them prepare for a successful and enjoyable learning experience.

SUPPORT FROM OTHER DEPARTMENTS

Develop a phased implementation plan to ensure some early successes.
Before designing your first live e-learning pilot project, plan time for
consultation discussions with your HR and IT departments.

Coordinating with the HR Department

In some companies, training program results must be tracked and
reported to HR for performance and/or compliance tracking purposes.
Avoid problems later by working out tracking and reporting processes
during your pilot project.

Coordinating with the IT Department

It is important to talk with your IT department to determine the capabilities of your company's technical resources.

- If you are purchasing and installing virtual classroom software
  on your corporate network, the support and cooperation of your
  IT department will be critical.

- If you are using a hosted virtual classroom solution, the IT
  Department will still need to be kept informed and they might
  have questions regarding bandwidth, firewalls, security, and client software installations on employee computers.

Work with IT to provide administration and support for your virtual
classroom solution—you want them as allies, not enemies, to your
training plans. Finally, you will need to talk with your Webmaster
about website requirements to support your virtual classroom program.

TECHNICAL SUPPORT

Put in place an effective technical support system for instructors and
first time attendees in your virtual classroom program. Here are some
tasks to include in your technical support plan.

Procedures for instructors:

- Give instructors written procedures for setting up the course, developing and loading course materials, presentation files/ slides, polls, quizzes, and assessments.

- Provide guidelines for how multi-media features can be used if your virtual classroom supports this function.

- List procedures for using application sharing and web tour features of the software.

- Communicate procedures for managing class enrollment—this includes e-mail communication with students confirming enrollment, reminders for classes, and class updates information.

- Provide guidelines for how to use the reporting functions to generate enrollment reports, attendance, and testing results reports.

- List procedures for schedule class sessions and rehearsals.

Technical support for instructors:

- Provide contact person(s) for technical support for course material development.

- Provide contact person(s) for technical support with virtual classroom operations.

- Provide a procedure to refer a student for technical support when they encounter technical difficulties coming to class or during a class session.

When conducting a class, instructors are not expected to provide technical support to participants. They should be familiar with the typical types of technical problems participants might experience, but they should refer the student to a support person for assistance. When conducting the first class of a new course, it is a good idea to set up a second audio conference call for technical support. When a participant indicates they are having technical difficulty, the instructor can immediately give that participant the technical support conference call number or have the operator transfer them to the technical support conference call. A support person can work with the participant to resolve the issues without disrupting the entire class or delaying the start. When the problem is resolved, the participant is transferred back into the regular class.

First level support for virtual classroom participants:

Attending a virtual classroom training session may be a new experience for employees. Virtual classroom products have matured and are user friendly. With a minimum of effort on the participant's part to do a *self-check* of equipment and connection, most first time attendees can successfully join a class. The most common technical problem for first time attendees is NOT READING THE INSTRUCTIONS. So, the first level of technical support is a phone number to reach a patient and friendly person who can answer questions and guide people through the log-on process.

Staff providing first level support should also be aware of common technical issues—browser versions, browser settings, and plug-in or client software installation issues. Handling the multi-tasking involved in designing and conducting a live session requires quick thinking and thorough familiarity with the process. As your company develops the internal procedures to offer first level support, you can ask your virtual classroom vendor for help. Most vendors provide training for this type of technical support in a half a day. First level support staff must be trained and knowledgeable about these typical technical issues.

Second level support for virtual classroom participants:

On occasion, a first time participant may encounter technical problems with a computer or the company's firewall or proxy server. Make sure that you have a system in place to handle these second level support issues. Typically these issues are referred to the organization's help desk or IT Department. Your vendor's technical support department might also serve as a back-up resource, based on the licensing agreement.

Be sure to log all technical problems during your pilot live e-learning project and develop a list of frequently encounter technical assistance problems. This data will help you refine an effective and cost efficient technical support system for your live e-learning program.

Setting up the support systems for a virtual training program is similar to selecting the facility for a face-to-face training program. When you contract with a hotel for meeting space for a face-to-face training program, you are considering much more than just price. Your selection of a hotel includes a range of criteria including location, room setup, audiovisual support, catering, and the hotels reputation on providing service. Your experience has taught you that all of these factors are important in creating an environment for your training to be successful.

Moving to a virtual training environment requires the same level of support and attention to details. The shift is in who provides these services. Rather than contracting with a hotel, your organization will now have the responsibility to make sure that these important support services are provided *in house*.

COOKBOOK QUESTION

As you begin to develop the plans for implementing your pilot virtual classroom program, what are the key learner and instructor support issues you will have to address?

Coordination across departments:

Technical support:

8
Going Forward

In *The Live E-learning Cookbook,* we have provided you with basic information on how the live virtual classroom can be used to meet three key business challenges:

Time to Market—How rapidly can I deploy new products?

Time to Productivity—How rapidly can I deploy new skills?

Time to Knowledge—How rapidly can I disseminate information?

We hope you have found this book to be an easy-to-follow guide and reference to help you create scalable, systematic, and sustainable virtual classroom programs. Your next step is to take what you have learned and put it into practice. Here are a few key summary thoughts to guide you as you move forward using the live virtual classroom.

- **Define the business objective for your e-learning project:** For your project to be successful, it is important that you have a clear understanding of your business and training outcomes.

- **Live e-learning is not just for the tech-savvy:** Many beginners think that e-learning is only suitable for teaching IT courses to the tech-savvy. Hopefully, the case scenarios have demonstrated the wide range of business learning issues that can be addressed cost and time effectively with the use of the virtual classroom.

- **Choose your technology provider carefully:** For companies that are just beginning to explore the virtual classroom, consider the option of using a hosted virtual classroom provider. This approach enables you to minimize your startup technology investment and means short lead-time in setting up your virtual classroom.

- **Evaluate your pilot e-learning projects:** Be sure to include your evaluation measurements so you can measure success and ROI on your e-learning project. Facts, figures, and ROI help you build the case for wider application of e-learning in your organization. Evaluation will ensure that you have a process to identify strengths and weakness, allowing you to continually improve and develop your project.

- **Focus on the learning outcomes as you develop your training content:** Do not allow yourself to get distracted by the technology. Technology does not equal learning. Creating the learning opportunity for your employees is based on how your instructors use the technology to provide compelling and highly interactive learning opportunities.

- **Build engagement into your learning programs:** As with any learning or training program, ensure that the employee is actively engaged with the subject and is connecting with the learning. We have laid out a number of instructional strategies that you can use to design, rehearse, and deliver your live e-learning programs.

On a final note, we would like to share with you the story of how this book was written. Our work together writing this book was completed entirely through virtual collaboration between four geographically dispersed authors (Hawaii, California, Florida, and Maryland). We found that the virtual classroom and collaboration technology we used with our clients was fully robust enough to support our collaboration writing this book.

Our paths initially crossed in a series of professional connections as we networked and collaborated on various projects. Friendships strengthened as we shared common interests, strategies, and techniques for virtual classroom instruction. On occasion, several of us collaborated on consulting engagements.

The live e-learning cookbook project started with an initial conference call where we explored the idea of working together to write this book. That conference call was followed by a series of document conference meetings where we shared ideas, defined our audience, and developed the outline for the book. We created idea papers and shared documents back and forth by email.

It was at this point that we learned about newly released collaborative software. We each subscribed to the software and created a 'shared space' to consolidate the growing volume of documents. We used the application for storing and sharing documents, and managing versions of chapter drafts. We also used the threaded discussion features to keep minutes of our online meetings and the calendar function for scheduling our conference calls.

During the course of our working together, we scheduled numerous online meetings using and sampling different virtual e-learning products. The technology chapter summarizes the features and functions and the results of our product exploration. We have watched these products improve as new versions are released and the virtual classroom product area matured.

The four of us never had the opportunity to meet and work together face-to-face in the same room during this project. However, we did manage to connect in person on occasion. Conferences were the logical place to meet. Jim and Kat jointly presented at an ASTD conference. Al and Jim met at Training 2002. Our paths have also crossed at the TechLearn and Online Learning conferences. We arranged our schedules to meet at Online Learning in September 2001, but 9-11 forced us to cancel our of travel plans. We continued to collaborate virtually.

Coming down the home stretch of editing this book, we moved to a simpler technology—the editor features of word processing. As the final copies of the manuscript came together, full draft copies were circulated via email for comments and editing. As this book goes to press, we will all miss our Friday conference calls. Collaborating on this book has been an exciting and wonderful experience for all four of us. We have stimulated each other's thinking and writing, our friendships have grown and, most importantly, we trust that our collaboration will benefit you, the reader, as you venture into the world of live e-learning.

Let us know about your successes with the virtual classroom. We would love to hear about how you were able to use the ideas and e-learning recipes in this book to shorten your learning curve and rapidly achieve success with your virtual classroom initiatives.

Author Biographies

KATHLEEN (KAT) BARCLAY, PH.D.

Dr. Barclay co-founded Strategic Visions in 1991 to assist companies and individuals eager to maximize technology. She now directs The Center for IntentionaLearning, a partner company that focuses on innovative online business coaching and training services designed to improve business performance. As an acknowledged expert since 1996 in live e-learning development and implementation, she uses web conferencing to help companies, teams, and individuals achieve desired personal and professional performance results.

Kat gained extensive experience in sales, human resources, training, and corporate management working for various global high-technology companies for over 25 years. She pioneered multiple international distance-delivery programs, including initiation of a worldwide satellite network and innovative implementations of video, CBT, and web-based training. This combination of expertise in business and technology has led to the production of online workshops for a range of small firms to Fortune 500 companies. Topics include the facilitation of strategic planning, delivery of new product introductions via the Web, coaching entrepreneurs, training instructors in successful online presentation, and the effective management of virtual workgroups.

A Ph.D. in Organizational Systems Psychology, her ground-breaking research in the field of online, live instruction is referenced internationally. Dr. Barclay is a recognized conference speaker, contributing author, associations Board Member, and online professor for international universities.

KBarclay@IntentionaLearning.com
www.IntentionaLearning.com

AL GORDON

Al is a Program Manager for the Customer Service organization at Cisco Systems, Inc., San Jose, California and is part of a team that is responsible for Customer Service and Internet Commerce tools training. Prior to his current position Al was E-Learning Programs Manager for the Knowledge Management and Delivery Group at Cisco. He is also currently a doctoral candidate at Nova Southeastern University, pursuing a Ph.D. in Computer and Information Science, specializing in the application of technology to learning, knowledge and performance improvement.

Prior to his work with Cisco, Al worked for Siemens Information and Communication Networks where he developed and managed the Siemens Virtual University, which delivered live e-learning training programs for over 40,000 employees and customers. He has spoken extensively at technology and training industry conferences about live e-learning, and has been interviewed by a number of technology and training publications with regards to live e-learning implementation and management.

algordon@cisco.com
www.cisco.com

JIM HOLLAHAN

Jim, an expert in e-learning, helps organizations build effective professional development and in-service training programs. He is president of Essential Solutions, Inc. (ESI), a Silver Spring, Maryland, based consulting company.

Jim began his training career working for associations including serving seven years as the national program director for United Cerebral Palsy Associations. Jim is a pioneer in the distance education field, implementing his first live audio teleconference training program in 1987. Over 20,000 UCP staff, families, and volunteers participated in national best practice distance seminars.

Jim formed ESI in 1998 to help organizations harness the power, convenience and cost effectiveness of distance audio and web conferencing. Building community is a part of Jim's personal mission statement and is reflected in Essential Solutions way of doing business. ESI has developed unique and specialized expertise in live, facilitated, interactive web presentations, seminars, and meetings.

ESI helps organizations plan and pilot live e-learning programs and trains staff and subject matter experts in the skills and techniques required to conduct quality web meetings and presentations. Successful ESI clients conduct their own collaborative web programs and seminars. ESI solutions have contributed to the success of e-learning programs at General Electric, Hewlett Packard, Siemens Business Communications, Sun Microsystems, Herman Miller, and IBM.
Hollahan@bellatlantic.net
www.esilearning.com

YATMAN LAI

Yatman is the Sr. Manager of eCommunities at Cisco Systems, responsible for the development and deployment of collaboration tools to support internal and external online communities such as the Network Professional Connection (**www.cisco.com/go/netpro**). Most recently, he was manager of Knowledge Management and Delivery responsible for the design, creation and distribution of systematic, scalable and sustainable learning and reference products. He created the successful ABCs of the *Cisco IOS—Understand the Essentials* series of multi-media learning programs.

Prior to Cisco, Yatman created the Learning Technology group at Siemens ICN, focusing on the large scale deployment of E-learning programs such as LearnTV (Live instructor-led training using video-conferencing technologies) and Siemens Virtual University (voice and data-conferencing). He has over 15 years of sales and line management experiences in multi-national corporations.
ylai@cisco.com
www.cisco.com

A few of the companies we have worked with:

Amadeus
Boeing
Cisco Systems
Council on Foundations
DataBeam Corporation
General Electric
Goldman Sachs
Hartford Technology Services
Herman Miller Inc
Hewlett Packard
Hills Pet Foods
IBM—Lotus Software Division
Intel
Prentke Romich Company
RWD Technologies
Siemens Business Communication Systems
Strayer University
Sun Microsystems, Inc.
Unisys
Siemens Medical
Siemens Automation
Siemens Information & Communications
University of Hawaii

www.ingramcontent.com/pod-product-compliance
Lightning Source LLC
Chambersburg PA
CBHW051242050326
40689CB00007B/1037